The Domestic Presidency:

Decision-Making in the White House

John H. Kessel
The Ohio State University

Duxbury Press
North Scituate, Massachusetts

Duxbury Press

A DIVISION OF WADSWORTH PUBLISHING COMPANY, INC.

The Domestic Presidency: Decision-Making in the White House was edited and prepared for composition by Katharine G. Tsioulcas. Interior design was provided by Jane Lovinger and the cover was designed by Brian Penry.

L.C. Cat. Card No.:
ISBN 0–87872–088–X
PRINTED IN THE UNITED STATES OF AMERICA

1 2 3 4 5 6 7 8 9 10—79 78 77 76 75

For My Father and the Memory of My Mother

Table of Contents

Preface

The purpose of this book is to reveal how domestic policy is formulated in the White House. The president himself makes the most important decisions, but scores of other persons gather the information he needs and make many vital decisions themselves. Who are those people? How do they spend their time? What does Washington look like from their perspective? What are their own attitudes about public policy, and how do those preferences affect the policies ultimately adopted by the administration? These are questions that need to be illuminated.

For some time now, presidential aides have been working not only in the White House proper but also in the Old Executive Office Building next door, the New Executive Office Building across Pennsylvania Avenue, and a number of smaller buildings nearby. Yet we know precious little about what they all do. Textbooks solemnly state that power has shifted from cabinet members to the National Security Council and the Domestic Council, and knowledgeable persons tell us that senior presidential aides outrank cabinet members in all but protocol, but the concrete facts to back up those assertions are not available. In contrast, we have some splendid studies on congressional committees by political scientists such as Richard Fenno, John Manley, and Charles Jones. As a result, we know much more about what takes place on Capitol Hill than we do about comparable events in the executive branch. Hopefully, this book will provide some of the information about one important group of presidential aides that we already have about many congressional committees.

The focus of the book is on the group, not on individuals. We are, after all, interested in the collective impact of the group on domestic policy, not in the isolated activities of single persons. This means we shall be using a language appropriate for group analysis. We shall be speaking of consensus, mean attitude scores, communication networks, and so forth, rather than discussing individual motivations, personality structures, and other concepts we would need for an analysis of individuals. Some of this may seem a little unfamiliar, but none of it is difficult to understand.

Three books were very important in my thinking about this group analysis of White House policy-making: *Labyrinths of Democracy: Adaptations, Linkages,*

Representation, and Policies in Urban Politics by Heinz Eulau and Kenneth Prewitt, *How Congressmen Decide: A Policy Focus* by Aage R. Clausen, and *The State of the Presidency* by Thomas E. Cronin. I had the privilege of reading these, one in page proof and two in manuscript, while I was planning the research for this book. The reader will find evidence of the influence of each. *Labyrinths of Democracy* suggested the importance of both the internal structure of political groups and the ways groups adapt to the environments in which they are situated. The discussion of policy areas was informed in crucial ways by Aage Clausen's work on congressional decision-making. Many ideas came from Thomas Cronin's new book on the presidency, the notion of a differentiated White House, an understanding of relationships between White House aides and others in the executive branch, and more.

Most of the information for this book was gathered in interviews with Domestic Council staff members in late 1972. Sixteen of the interviews took place in their offices, and four more were shorter telephone conversations. I promised the respondents that their anonymity would be protected, and I have used pseudonyms except for a very few cases where Kenneth R. Cole was speaking about how the work of the Domestic Council was organized. I have also changed the names of agencies and programs. The analytical point of each original statement has been retained, but the name of a similar agency or program has been substituted for that in the original conversation. If we are to learn more about the presidency — and we certainly need to do so — then those in the White House must feel they can speak candidly about their activities and be confident that scholars will handle that information in a responsible manner.

This book has very little to say about the events that have come to be called the Watergate affair. In a temporal sense the book was "pre-Watergate"; in fact, Chapters 2, 3, and 4 were in first draft before April, 1973, and they have not been changed in any substantial fashion. Why, the reader may ask, press on with an analysis that did not contain any direct evidence about Watergate? There are two reasons. One is that while a great deal of information has become available about Watergate, these revelations tell little about policy formulation. Those who wish a balanced view of the Nixon administration will want to consider the misdeeds of Watergate, but they should also consider what happened in relation to substantive policy. The second reason for publication is more fundamental. This information permits us to address questions that transcend Watergate. How can the presidency be organized to serve the interests of the president, particularly if he finds himself in an adverse power situation and cannot count on support from other political actors? How can staff support be arranged so the White House can act simultaneously in half a dozen policy areas? When authority to act in the name of the president is delegated, what happens to responsibility for the actions taken, and how can accountability be maintained? We shall not find any simple answers to these questions, but that is all the more reason for pondering them.

Finally, I should like to thank those who extended so much help to me. My chairman at Ohio State, Randall B. Ripley, thought I could make profitable use of a quarter's research leave. The findings from one National Science Foundation grant (GS-2660) were instrumental in planning the research, and funds from another (GS-35084) covered some modest travel expenses. The Brookings Institution provided hospitality and a base in Washington by giving me Guest Scholar status. (I have, incidentally, been bemused by reports of hostile views of the Brookings Institution harbored by the Nixon White House. All my requests for interviews were sent on Brookings letterheads, and I was very courteously received.) George Grassmuck was kind enough to put me in touch with Raymond K. Price, who made the invaluable suggestion that I should study the Domestic Council if I wanted to understand how administration policy was formulated. Kenneth R. Cole and many of his colleagues on the Domestic Council staff were good enough to make time in their busy schedules, and if I do not thank them by name, it is because I want to maintain the confidentiality I promised them. Thomas E. Cronin, Stephen Hess, and Charles O. Jones read an earlier draft, and made any number of helpful suggestions about ways in which improvements could be made. Robert Gormley of Duxbury Press was willing to act on his belief that the book ought to be published, and Katharine G. Tsioulcas and Jay P. Bartlett brought a facility of style and expression to the manuscript. If this book has merit, it is because all these kind people made it possible.

JOHN H. KESSEL

Columbus, Ohio
July 8, 1974

Chapter 1

Of Continuity and Change

The scene is familiar. Moments after noon on January 20, or at other times under emergency circumstances, the President-elect and the Chief Justice face each other. Both raise their right hands, and the oath is repeated. "I do solemnly swear that I will faithfully execute the Office of President of the United States, and will to the best of my Ability, preserve, protect and defend the Constitution of the United States." The names change. Harry S Truman. Dwight David Eisenhower. John Fitzgerald Kennedy. Lyndon Baines Johnson. Richard Milhous Nixon. Gerald R. Ford. But the oath is identical. The words are prescribed by the Constitution, and have been repeated by each of the 37 men who have entered the office.

What is true of the men and the oath they take is also true of the administrations they head. Of the elements that shape an administration, some are relatively fluid and some are relatively constant. Among the factors that are more likely to change from one administration to another are the character and work habits of the president himself, the power situation resulting from who controls what formal and informal power bases outside the White House, the attitudes of the voters as expressed in the election that put the president in office, and the men the president picks to occupy other important positions in his administration. Among the factors that are relatively stable are the policy areas with which the administration must deal, the complexity of the political environment, and the length of time available to the administration. Serious mistakes can be made by focusing only on either the relatively fluid considerations or only on those that are reasonably stable. The former could lead one to treat the presidency as a "plastic institution," to speak of the Kennedy administration, the Johnson administration, the Nixon administration, and their successors as distinctive entities, and to believe that such evanescent qualities as "style" and "tone" fully characterize an administration. Focusing on the constitutional stipulations and continuing problems could lead to the equally mistaken view that the human qualities of a president are inconsequential and that it doesn't make any difference who wins an election. A true appreciation of the presidency requires an understanding of how these several factors interact with one another. As is true of most human institutions, change and continuity are both present.

PRESIDENTIAL CHARACTER

James David Barber has told us much about the importance of presidential character, and the reader who wants to pursue this would be well advised to turn to his book.[1] In his usage, character and style are interrelated. *Character* refers to the underlying personality, the way the president orients himself toward life, while *style* denotes the president's habitual ways in rhetoric, personal relations, and homework. These working habits are important because the president's preferences are reflected in the way the White House is organized and conducts its business. For example, Harry Truman believed in direct talk with those who were loyal to him, and was willing to make decisions on the spot when matters were brought to him. His White House was organized relatively informally, with the president himself presiding over morning meetings of his top aides. Dwight Eisenhower entered the White House believing it could be organized far more efficiently. He added an assistant to the president to oversee staff operations, staff backup for the National Security Council, a secretary for the White House staff to keep track of decisions that needed to be made, and a small secretariat for the cabinet. The result was a White House ability to respond rapidly to queries, and time for Eisenhower himself to focus on international matters of concern to him. John Kennedy brought with him detachment, wit, and a desire for information that bore on the decisions he would have to make. His staff was organized less formally, as the president liked to deal directly with the persons responsible for handling the matter being decided. Lyndon Johnson was anything but detached about himself. He had an abundant energy, and tended to overpower other people when he came in contact with them. His knowledge of others and how they would react was of less value in the White House than it had been in the Senate, where there were votes to be lined up, but he still wanted to be at the center of things and be able to communicate to others the urgency he felt himself. Richard Nixon, as his Republican predecessor, believed in delegation. He tended to rely on relatively few aides he believed to be loyal to him, and liked to have detailed recommendations submitted on paper so he could ponder them at his leisure. That meant a return to formal organization and decentralization in the Nixon White House.

POWER SITUATION

Charles O. Jones tells us there are some ten political conditions inside and outside Congress that significantly affect the behavior of the minority party in Congress.[2] These include such matters as the relative strength of the minority party, national party unity, presidential power, majority party leadership and organization, size of the margin separating the majority and minority parties, and so forth. Obviously, there is a parallel set of political conditions that affect the behavior of an administration. First of all, what is the situation on Capitol Hill? Does his party control both branches of Congress, or a single branch, or are both the House and Senate in the hands of the opposition? How many members in either branch are sympathetic to the programs the president intends to present? How skillful are the House and Senate leaders of his party, and how disposed are they to put their weight behind the president's program? Second, are the courts likely to rule that the president may legally do what he wants to do? There have been times when presidential action was inhibited by the Supreme Court. A prime example is that of Franklin D. Roosevelt's first term. He had not had an opportunity to make any judicial appointments, and many New Deal initiatives were ruled unconstitutional. Conversely, by his third term he was able to count on a court majority if any of his actions should be subject to legal challenge. Third, how supportive is the bureaucracy likely to be? The professionals in virtually every agency are interested in expanding the activity in which they are engaged. If a president comes into office seeking to increase the scope of governmental activity, it is a relatively easy matter for him to find allies in the various departments and agencies. If, on the other hand, a president wants to cut government spending in order to reduce taxes, it would be unrealistic to expect many bureau chiefs to journey to Capitol Hill to plead with Congress to cut their budgets. Finally, how are the president's relations with the mass media? If the president has the gift of tongues, if he is willing to take the time to prepare for public and private sessions with reporters, and if his policy initiatives can be successfully explained to editorial writers, the administration may be sustained by support from the media — at least for a while. Every recent president has had his share of criticism from this "Fourth Branch of Government,"[3] but the amount of support for an administration is important in sustaining it in adversity. The commentary of the press is important for many reasons, but two stand out. Newspaper and television commentary is the most immediate feedback received by an administration when it begins on an endeavor. And newspapers, especially the *New York Times* and the *Washington Post* (because they are morning papers read on the way to work), form an important part of the internal communication network in Washington itself.

With this many conditions included in the "power situation," one can think of a fair number of combinations. Perhaps the effect of the power situation on the administration could be better understood by asking about the nature of these circumstances after Lyndon Johnson's election in 1964 and after Richard Nixon's in 1968. In the case of President Johnson, he had large majorities in both the House and Senate, including quite a few Northern Democrats who had been elected for the first time in 1964. The Warren Court had a liberal majority. The bureaucrats saw 1965 as a chance to obtain legislative authorization for activities in which they had wanted to engage for some time, and both the *Washington Post* and the *New York*

TABLE 1-1
Factors Affecting Administration Behavior

Relatively Fluid Factors	Relatively Constant Factors
Character and work habits of president	Policy areas
Power situation outside White House	Complexity of political environment
Attitudes and skills of persons in responsible positions	Political calendar
Attitudes of voters	

Times had supported President Johnson in his bid for re-election. Now consider the case of Richard Nixon when he took office. Both houses of Congress had fairly substantial opposition majorities, and Richard Nixon had campaigned against some of the holdings of the Supreme Court. The bureaucracy was unlikely to produce many suggestions about ways federal activities could be turned back to the states or to private enterprise, and the endorsement of Hubert Humphrey by the *New York Times* and *Washington Post* was a fair indicator of their editorial stance. It doesn't take much reflection to see that the power situation was far more favorable for the incoming Johnson administration than for the incoming Nixon administration.

ATTITUDES OF THE VOTERS
AND OF STAFF MEMBERS

The goals of an administration are going to be affected by the personal goals of the president as well as by the power situation in which he finds himself. They will be further determined by the wishes of the public as expressed in the most recent election, and by the type of persons appointed to principal positions in the administration. Of particular importance here are the attitudes of the voters and the attitudes of the staff members involved in making policy decisions. There are some interaction effects between these two sets of attitudes (How do the staff members know what the attitudes of the public are? What effect does this knowledge have on their own attitudes about what is desirable public policy?), and this is a question that we shall want to examine. For the moment, it is enough for us to be aware that these attitudes are related to the goals sought by an administration, and that they are among the factors that do change from administration to administration.

POLICY AREAS

There are also factors that are reasonably stable from administration to administration. Among these are the problems with which presidents must deal, the kinds of politics they typically employ when they deal with them, the resources at their disposal for this purpose, and the speed or reticence with which they address them. These are not completely stable (any more than, say, the attitudes of the voters are identical from one election to the next), but a study of the Truman, Eisenhower, Kennedy, and Johnson administrations shows that six different policy areas can be discerned, and all four administrations have shown similar tendencies in dealing with these policy areas.[4]

The most important issue area is *international involvement*. More than any other area, the major activity here takes place within the executive branch. Many agencies take part in the traditional diplomacy of negotiation, and the newer diplomacy of foreign aid, information exchange, and presidential travel. The armed forces provide strength for negotiating positions, and, if all else fails, military power which can be committed to battle.

International involvement is an imperative policy area, one to which the president must respond (and, obviously, one in which the foreign participants are not subject to his control). In recent decades international affairs have commanded more of a president's time and attention as his tenure in the White House progressed. Attention to this area builds during the first term, drops as re-election year comes around, and then becomes even more prominent during his second term. This pattern suggests these responsibilities are sufficiently compelling that a president pays increasing attention to national security affairs, whether he comes to office with long experience or personal interest in foreign policy, as Dwight Eisenhower and Richard Nixon, or whether his prior career has been more concerned with domestic affairs, as was the case with Harry Truman and Lyndon Johnson.

Perhaps most important, the politics of international involvement are primarily symbolic. Even during the Cold War era, positive symbolic references ("America stands for the best hopes of mankind.") were far more frequent than recourse to military activity. This reflects not only preferences but also the limits to American resources. When measured against other policy areas, expenditures on national security have been very high. When measured, however, against the range of our international commitments, American resources are finite indeed.[5] Hence, the majority of our interventions must be symbolic.

The other imperative policy area in which the president must take action is *economic management*. This concerns not only the obvious elements of fiscal and monetary policy but also employment, labor relations, and such economic infrastructure matters as transportation. While purely economic concerns are part of the activity characteristic of this policy area, it is better conceptualized as resource management in a very broad sense.

Presidents are drawn into this area of activity by outside stimuli rather than by a fixed relation to the political calendar. If the economy is faltering, the government is going to be concerned about rising unemployment and falling tax receipts. Equally obviously, if there is a serious inflation problem, a president feels called upon to try to slow down a rapidly rising cost of living. Another stimulus to presidential action, perhaps less apparent, is a conflict between two rival economic groupings, such as business and labor. If the rivals are deadlocked, each has a desire to bring government in on its side.

The politics of economic management are regulatory politics. Rules are promulgated; parties are told they may and may not do things. This may suggest why a president prefers to avoid this policy area unless he is forced into it. If businessmen are told they may not raise prices, or labor unions are told they may not engage in a particular bargaining practice, they are not going to be happy with the president associated with this policy. Accordingly, presidents will act in this policy area, but before they do so, the economic perils and adverse political consequences must be clear enough to outweigh the political costs of taking action.

The third policy area is the distribution of *social benefits*. This involves conferring benefits on individuals (actually, classes of individuals) to shelter them from some of life's adversities. Housing programs, educational subsidies, aid to dependent children, medical benefits, and veterans' programs are all examples of programs falling into this policy area. Often a single population grouping is the object of this policy. They make what the administration regards as a legitimate claim, and the president asks Congress for legislation to give some benefit to them.

The politics of allocation, "give-away programs" in the language of critics, is a popular business. If a president runs the risk of losing friends through regulation, it is relatively easy for him to make friends by distributing benefits.

The temporal pattern in this policy area is just the opposite of that in international involvement. The distribution of social benefits is primarily a first-term phenomenon. Attention to social benefits rises gradually, then becomes *the* most important concern during a president's fourth year in office. Once he has been re-elected, presidential concern with this form of allocative politics is apt to drop sharply. Presidents tend to distribute largess when they have the greatest need to increase their own political support.

TABLE 1-2
Presidential Policy Areas

Name of Policy Area	Type of Politics	Importance	Imperative
International involvement	Symbolic	Major	Yes
Economic management	Regulatory	Major	Yes
Social benefits	Allocative	Major	No
Civil liberties	Symbolic & Regulatory	Minor	No
Natural resources	Regulatory	Minor	No
Agriculture	Allocative	Minor	No

The remaining three policy areas are substantially less important than international involvement, economic management, or social benefits, but they still merit attention. In recent decades the area of civil liberties has been dominated by the struggle of minority groups for civil rights, but it also includes the great constitutional guarantees such as free speech and due process. Nor should it be forgotten that all governments have sought to insure domestic tranquillity. Indeed, references to the need to protect personal security can be traced from the ancient "extension of the King's peace" to modern "law-and-order" themes.

It might seem redundant to refer to the politics of civil liberties as the politics of justice, but the concept of equity is essential to understanding this policy area. The tendency has been to rely on symbols and regulation in about equal measure. Regulations in such controversial areas as civil rights are most likely to be accepted if they are explained as applications of more general rights of citizens, or understood as privileges granted to all persons under the Constitution. Appeals to fairness on behalf of all people are most likely to be honored when they are backed by the force of law. One without the other is insufficient; both together give some hope of success in dealing with these delicate issues. The temporal pattern in this policy area has been very slight, but it can be detected. Presidents have been most apt to move on these issues just after their elections, presumably because of commitments made in the course of their campaigns.

The politics of natural resources and the politics of agriculture can both be thought of as special cases of policy areas already described, with particular sets of issues and actors. Natural resources is closely related to economics; if one thinks of the latter in the broad sense of resource management, the relationship is quite clear. And the issues that recently have animated this policy area — recreation areas, pollution control, energy needs — are certainly related to population growth. Both the behavioral and temporal patterns, regulation when necessary and sporadic presidential attention as a function of long-range developments, bear a strong resemblance to economic management.

The final policy area, agricultural politics, is a special case of the distribution of social benefits. The beneficiary groups have been farmers, specifically farmers producing any of the six "basics," wheat, corn, dairy products, cotton, tobacco, and peanuts. This has not been the only agricultural program, but those producers have been cushioned against adversity by subsidy programs for the last four decades. The dominant temporal pattern in this policy area has been long-range. Agricultural politics has tended to recede in importance as farmers have become less numerous. If, however, farmers continue to lose political power and consumer groups continue to grow as a political force, agricultural politics may well become more akin to economic management, with the government as the arbiter between powerful contenders.

COMPLEXITY OF POLITICAL ENVIRONMENT

The power situation outside the White House may favor one administration and inhibit another, but the number of persons, groups, and institutions with which the

White House must deal is a fact all administrations must face. It would be somewhat inaccurate to refer to this as an unchanging consideration. The political environment has been growing steadily more complex as American society has been growing more complex and creating new interests and institutions in the process. No recent president has had the freedom of time and action provided by a simple environment.

One way to understand this is to think about the number of actors involved in a single policy matter. Take food costs. To begin with, this is no longer confined to the Department of Agriculture. The State, Treasury, and Commerce Departments are immediately involved, because many of our agricultural sales are overseas and thus affect our foreign relations, balance-of-payments problem, and foreign trade. The Department of Health, Education and Welfare is concerned, because rising food costs will affect the school lunch program and the adequacy of welfare payments. The Labor Department knows that an increase in the cost of living is going to produce pressures for pay increases when new contracts are negotiated. And so on. Within the Department of Agriculture itself, many bureaus have activities that concern economic affairs — the Farmers Home Administration, the Farmer Cooperative Service, the Commodity Exchange Authority, the Consumer and Marketing Service, the Packers and Stockyards Administration, the Economic Research Service, the Foreign Economic Development Service, the Statistical Reporting Service, the Agricultural Research Service, the Agricultural Stabilization and Conservation Service, the Export Marketing Service, the Federal Crop Insurance Corporation, and the Foreign Agricultural Service.

On Capitol Hill there are the House and Senate Agriculture Committees, which frame agricultural authorization bills, but there are also the House and Senate Appropriations Committees (or, more exactly, the Agriculture subcommittees), which must approve any spending called for by the authorization bills. Any bill coming from the House committees moves to the floor through the House Rules Committee, and if the bill was sufficiently important to be part of the administration's legislative program, it would be considered by the party leadership as well.

Serious attempts at legislation, and the implementation of any law that was passed, would gain the attention of a number of interest groups. The "peak groups" in agriculture, those that embrace wider interests than, say, corn or beef production, include the American Farm Bureau Federation, the National Farmers Union, the National Grange, the National Conference of Commodity Organizations, and the National Farm Organization. These interest groups would speak for producers, while distributors would be represented by other organizations, and recently organized consumers' groups would be quite vocal about the need to keep food prices down.[6]

Messages coming from party leaders would be somewhat broader, but they would be most likely to depend on the constituencies the leaders represented. Given the present concentration of the American population in metropolitan areas, they would be most likely to urge that something be done to keep prices down. Those from producing areas, however, could be expected to reflect an opposite point of view. The net impact of the political party on such an issue would probably reflect party structure. The crucial questions would be who in the party was recognized as having particular expertise on this question, and what the relations of these persons happened to be to the next scheduled elections.

Nor should it be forgotten that all of the national organizations we have been discussing have state and local counterparts. States have their own departments of agriculture, and there are extension agents active at the county level. Senators and congressmen make frequent trips to their home constituencies, and many keep district offices open. The interest groups tend to have their members concentrated in certain areas of the country, but where they are active, they are organized right down to the county level. Elections, of course, are held in states and their subdivisions. Candidates for state legislature and county commissioner can be affected by shifts in public opinion growing out of changes in food costs just as much as congressmen and United States senators.

From the White House point of view, in other words, there are many bases that need to be touched on any single issue. Now if the reader will think about the number of issues that come along in each issue area, and further recall that there are six principal issue areas, and multiply the number of actors mentioned in this single example by the total number of issues with which a president must deal, he will have a fair idea of the complexity of the political environment.

POLITICAL CALENDAR

There is more than one political calendar that affects administration behavior. The first is the annual pattern that is fixed by the requirements for submission of the State of the Union message, the budget, and the economic message at the beginning of the legislative year in January.[7] This means that an annual program cycle will begin sometime after Labor Day when programs to be proposed to Congress in the coming year are being readied. Fall is probably the time of the heaviest work load for the policy staffers in the White House, because work is still progressing on Capitol Hill on the present year's program at the same time preparations for the next year are being made. If it is an odd year, some legislation will still be in committee while other bills have reached the floor. If it is an even year, Congress will be racing to adjourn so the members can get back home to campaign. In election years, major bills will be on the floor just before adjournment, following which there will be a rapid shift of focus onto the campaign, so any real attention to the legislative program for the coming year gets deferred until November and December. The Christmas season is a time for basic decisions about the budget for the coming fiscal year and the accompanying legislative program. From January through March, work is concentrated on the specifics of new programs. The three required statements (State of the Union, budget, and economic message) inaugurate the "message season," during which a series of special messages go to Capitol Hill, each concerning action desired in some particular area. At the same time a good many meetings are being held between White House staffers, persons from the departments concerned with the programs, senators and congressmen, and interest group representatives. These meetings continue during the spring as the White House urges the merits of its programs on the Congress. By June (especially in an odd year) the pressure of work with Congress eases off a bit. In August Congress takes its annual vacation. This is also likely to be vacation time at the White House, both for the president, who is likely to be at a "Summer White House" somewhere, and for aides, who get away for a rest while they have a chance. Those who remain in Washington take the opportunity to make preparations for the coming year's legislative program, since the cycle starts over again after Labor Day.

The longer sequence resulting from the schedule of elections is superimposed onto this annual pattern. Congressional elections come every two years, and presidential every four, but as long as our presidents have some chance of being elected for a second term, the underlying periodicity is eight years. (There is also the odd year-even year distinction resulting from congressional elections every other year, but that has just been described.) A newly elected president may expect a honeymoon period, during which he enjoys wide public support and Congress is responsive to his suggestions. The chances of congressional support, of course, will be particularly good if he has been elected by a wide margin and a number of congressmen credit the president with some responsibility for their own election. Yet if we look closely, we see that the new president is not yet ready to take advantage of this favorable political environment. The presidency is an extraordinarily complex job, and new officeholders are rarely ready to cope with all of its challenges. The result is that behind seeming decisiveness lies a good deal of trial-and-error learning on the part of new administrations.[8] The period of initial learning takes about eighteen months, by which time the president has to accept whatever he has obtained from his first Congress, and turn hopefully to the midterm elections. The third year of an administration is the best time for accomplishment in the first term. The president and his aides are by now relatively experienced, and they may be able to obtain some important legislation if it is of a character that can be got through in the first session of the new Congress. The fourth year, of course, is a year when partisanship becomes dominant, and both administration and opposition try their best to present a case that will win votes. Because of its greater visibility, the president's own record is likely to be central in a re-election campaign. If he is returned to office by a sizable vote, and if a congressional majority of his own party is elected at the same time, the fifth and sixth years provide the best opportunity for real accomplishment. Again the president has a period in which he can count on support, but this time the president, his key aides, department heads, and other important administration figures should know what they are about. (The most prolific legislative sessions of recent decades took place in 1965–66, when a just re-elected Lyndon Johnson had a substantial Democratic majority.) The seventh and eighth years are characteristically marked by continuation rather than innovation. As the administration comes to a close, it becomes increasingly difficult for a president to recruit new talent to replace departing personnel. Assistant secretaries are promoted to secretary, and the administration stays on its already charted course as politicians turn their attention to the choice of the next president.

Beyond the annual cycle and the election cycle, there are the periodicities already noted in certain policy areas. International involvement is likely to command most of a president's attention, but particularly so during a second term. Social benefits are most attended to when a president is running for re-election, and civil rights promises fulfilled after election campaigns. Hence, there appear to be three relatively fixed patterns that together make up the political calendar. The annual decision cycle is the most evident, but the annual cycle, the election calendar, and temporal characteristics of the policy areas all delimit a president's opportunities and thus affect administration behavior.

SOME PRELIMINARY COMPARISONS

The argument is that it is the *combined effects* of these factors that shape what happens when an administration is in office. Each of them — the character and work habits of the president, the power situation, the attitudes of the voters as expressed in the most recent election, the attitudes of the men who are appointed to key positions, the policy areas, the complexity of the environment, and the political calendar — undoubtedly has some individual impact. But our real interest is in interaction effects: for example, the effects of the complexity of the political environment as that interacts with each of these other features. Are the president's work habits such that he copes easily with complexity? Are the attitudes of his key aides such that they are frustrated by the political environment or take it as a challenge to be mastered? And so on.

Consider the effects of these matters with respect to the Johnson and Nixon administrations. Lyndon Johnson and Richard Nixon were very different men; the former directly and personally concerned with many details, the latter one who relied very heavily on aides. (One small example. When Lyndon Johnson selected Hubert Humphrey to be his running mate in 1964, Humphrey was summoned from the Democratic convention in Atlantic City and flown to Washington. When he arrived at the White House he was personally greeted by President Johnson, who, with his arm about Humphrey's shoulder, said, "Hubert, how would you like to be my vice president?" When Richard Nixon selected Gerald Ford as his vice president-designate, he telephoned the congressman, told him, "Al has something to tell you," and then turned the phone over to chief of staff Alexander Haig. Just imagine Lyndon Johnson turning a chore of this kind over to an aide!) The power situation was vastly more favorable to President Johnson when he was sworn in on

January 20, 1965, than it was for President Nixon four years later. The cabinet members and White House aides selected by President Johnson were somewhat more liberal than those chosen by President Nixon. The mood of the voters who elected Richard Nixon was slightly less favorable to further expansion of the federal government and further advances in civil rights, and certainly less supportive of American involvement in Vietnam, than had been the case when Lyndon Johnson had been re-elected in the mid-sixties. If these factors varied, then it is well to remember that both presidents had to deal with the same problems — Vietnam, inflation, the cities, desegregation, and the like. Further, they faced equally complex environments and were allotted the same four years from election to election.

The continuity between the Nixon and Ford administrations may be traced to the similarity in factors affecting them. President Ford's statement of his own views, "I would say that I am a moderate on domestic issues, a conservative in fiscal affairs, and a dyed-in-the-wool internationalist in foreign affairs," could be taken as a fair description of the attitudes of Richard Nixon, leading members of the Nixon administration, and the voters who put them in office. Moreover, the power situation outside the White House was just about the same; there had not been an election before the Ford administration took office; and the other factors that normally produce stability — the similarity of the policy areas, the complexity of the political environment, and the fixed political calendar — did so.

The variations between the Nixon and Ford administrations came from differences in the characters and work habits of the two men, and the skills of their principal appointees. Not only was President Ford much more open and direct, but whereas President Nixon had a strong preference for having arguments submitted on paper, Mr. Ford was more of a listener and a talker. One who watched President Ford at close range described his decision-making pattern this way:

> *You hear these things about President Ford not doing any reading. Don't you believe it! I remember very early in his administration, they gave him a thick notebook filled with facts about the American economy. The next day he knew every single thing that was in that book. It's just that he's much more interested in having a group sit down around a table and talk things out. He wants proper briefing beforehand, of course, but with that he will raise questions and make up his own mind as he listens to others express their views.*

The Domestic Council was retained in the Ford administration. As Counsel to the President Philip Buchan explained: "You have to keep the Council. . . . There are too many issues that involve two or more departments. I think you need a Domestic Council to mediate between the departments."[9] But it was all but inevitable that the way advice went from the Domestic Council to the president would be altered from the paper flow that marked the previous administration, and would accord with

Gerald Ford's habit of arriving at his own position while engaging in verbal give and take.

President Ford's selection of Nelson Rockefeller as vice president was also important in the administration's decision-making capability. As a long-time congressman, Gerald Ford was well accustomed to the House practice of making up one's mind through conversations with peers. Nelson Rockefeller, in contrast, brought executive experience gained in many federal positions and as governor of New York. When he took office in the Empire State, Rockefeller set up a series of task forces to study the state's problems, and his then secretary, Dr. William J. Ronan, created a program staff to provide liaison between the Governor's Office and the bureaucracy. The program associates, organized by functional areas in a manner not unlike the Nixon Domestic Council staff, refereed intramural disputes, sought out new program initiatives for the governor, and relayed the governor's wishes to those working in the agencies. Ideas developed by the task forces and the program staff often were adopted by Governor Rockefeller and his immediate advisors as they developed his legislative program.[10] As a result of this experience, Nelson Rockefeller's designation as vice president gave the Ford administration a capacity for systematic policy development and coordination.

Differences between the Nixon and Ford administrations also grew out of the interaction between the several factors we have been considering. Although the policy preferences of President Ford and his principal advisors were quite similar to those of their predecessors, they reacted in a very different way to the adverse power situation in which they found themselves. The most important changes were with respect to Congress and the media. Democratic majorities remained in both House and Senate, but President Ford had close personal friendships with the Democratic leaders as well as with his Republican colleagues. Most of the Washington press corps continued to be liberal, but Gerald Ford found it possible to chat easily with newsmen on some informal occasions. President Ford's principal liaison appointments helped with smooth relations. He kept experienced men in charge of the Congressional Liaison operation because he wanted men who were well regarded on Capitol Hill, and the Ford press secretaries, first Jerald ter Horst and then Ron Nessen, were highly respected as professional newsmen. The resulting changes in relationships between the White House and others in Washington did not resolve policy disputes about how problems should be dealt with, but they did promote an atmosphere in which Ford administration proposals could be viewed a little more sympathetically.

We can see another example of the combined effects of the seven factors if we look at the domestic policy staffs in the Johnson and Nixon administrations. The Johnson aides concerned with domestic policy were less formally organized. As Figure 1–1 suggests, some were working for Joseph Califano, the principal domestic aide (to the extent that one could be so designated), but others were being directed by Special Counsel Harry McPherson, Press Secretary Bill Moyers (who

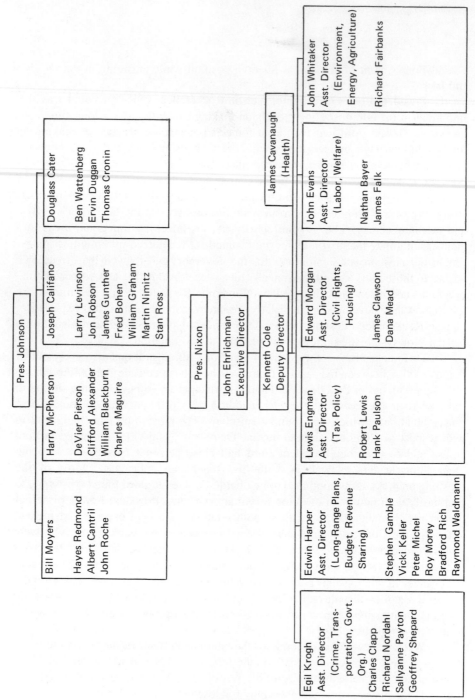

FIGURE 1–1

Comparison of Johnson and Nixon Domestic Policy Staffs

had some non-press responsibilities), and Douglass Cater, whose activities centered on relations with the Department of Health, Education and Welfare but who had some other tasks as well.[11] In the Johnson White House the person handling a particular assignment was likely to be the individual who was in the president's office when the subject came up. Richard Nixon organized his domestic staff along different lines. He could count on much less support outside the White House, and he needed a systematically organized staff within. The Nixon administration created a Domestic Council, and set up a staff to support it. John D. Ehrlichman was the executive director and Kenneth R. Cole, Jr., his deputy director, and everything was channeled through them.

Each of the assistant directors had a list of responsibilities, and when new tasks came along they were almost automatically referred to the "shop" headed by the appropriate assistant director. Perhaps most important, Mr. Nixon gave these aides considerable authority to act. As Kenneth Cole put it:

> *The president is a delegator* par excellence. *He delegates a lot of responsibility and authority, and John and I follow with that pattern. We depend on the staff to let us know things we should know about.*

Yet we should not overstate the differences between the two groups of policy aides. Both administrations had to deal with the same problems, and maintain liaison with the same outside groupings to do so. The number of people involved in the two groups was about the same. There were 20 staffers involved with domestic policy in the Johnson administration in 1967, and 28 persons (including administrative assistants to Ehrlichman and Cole who are not shown in Figure 1–1) assigned to the Domestic Council staff in late 1972. There were several journalists in the Johnson group and a couple more academics on the Nixon staff, but the most common background (about half in both cases) was law. Perhaps the most important link, though, is that both groups came to have similar views about the possibility of governing as a result of trying to deal with very similar problems and equally complex environments. Two Johnson aides told Thomas Cronin about the conclusions they had reached:

> *A program today often needs three or four departments and an equal number of congressional committees and subcommittees to even get things started. . . . There are just more and more people and more institutional drags involved. It takes time and testing to get things to work.*[12]

> *Except in times of emergencies, Presidents cannot get much accomplished . . . In some areas a President can have some psychological influence . . . for example, by speaking out on crime concerns. And in an eight-year period a President can start a shift of the budget and of the political system, but it takes a lot of pressure and a lot of time.*[13]

These thoughts about experience in trying to develop Great Society programs were not all that different from comments made by members of Richard
Nixon's Domestic Council staff:

> *I think that to an extent we tend to impose presidential priorities on the
> government, but I think there's a great limit on what we can do.*

> *There is the continuing problem of trying to strike a proper balance between
> the short-range brush fire problems that have to be taken care of and
> long-range problems that have to be given some attention as well. I think it's
> very easy for people's time to be siphoned off to day-to-day five-minute-
> attention-span kinds of problems. Now a person can argue you ought to
> spend most of your time on long-range planning, and worry about what's
> coming down the pike five years from now, but I don't think that's realistic.
> If you don't have a mechanism for taking care of the brush fire, short-range
> problems, those can sometimes build into the most troublesome problems
> you have to deal with.*

Either set of comments reveals a thoughtful analysis of the experience of working in
the White House, and both lead to the same conclusion. Regardless of the name of
the president, you try to further his initiatives, and to some extent you succeed. But
there are limits to what can be done. No president is able to command, and no
White House staff can simply issue orders to be obeyed. The environment is too
complex for that, but if one learns its intricacies well enough, and stays with
particular challenges long enough, some small victories can be won.

THE DEVELOPMENT OF A DIFFERENTIATED PRESIDENCY

To this point, our concern has been with similarities and differences from administration to administration. By shifting our time perspective from terms to decades,
though, we can use the same factors to cast some light on the long-term development of the presidency. Three of the considerations that were important in producing variation from one administration to another—the character and work habits of
presidents, the power situations in which they work, and the attitudes of the men
they appoint—do *not* have much impact on long-term institutional development,
for the simple reason that their effects are canceled out by short-term variation. If
several presidents in succession all worked in a relatively formal manner and all
faced adverse power situations, we would expect some consequences for institutional development. When one conducts his business informally and is favored by a
supportive power situation, and his successor is quite formal but limited by an
adverse power situation, we don't look for much continuing impact on the institution. For opposite reasons, we wouldn't expect the political calendar to affect the

evolution of the presidency. The fixed dates and terms constrain individual incumbents, but if we wish to explain how the presidency is different today from, say, the time Harry Truman returned to Independence, Missouri, we are not likely to find an answer in a fixed calendar.

The matters most likely to be related to long-range change are those that are slowly evolving: the attitudes of the voters about the kinds of activities and programs that they deem appropriate for the federal government; the policy areas, as they reflect the ascent to political power of new population groupings and the decline in importance of shrinking groupings; and the complexity of the political environment with which each administration must cope. Each of these has been moving in the direction of increased complexity. Regardless of the particular cause one chooses, and regardless of whether attention is directed to the international scene or to domestic affairs, the answer is the same: more interests, more agencies, more programs with more ties between the programs, and more work to be done in order to "take care that the laws be faithfully executed."

This explanation of increasing social and governmental complexity may or may not be correct, but the fact of a growing presidency is indisputable. Many administrations could be cited as those in which growth was "begun": the McKinley administration, which ended the weak presidency era following Lincoln; the Roosevelt-Taft-Wilson progressive period, in which a number of new programs were begun; the Harding administration, which saw the origin of the Bureau of the Budget and of the presidential budget process. Any of these would be correct in the sense that there were activities begun, and the presidency is much more complex now than when the incumbent in question was in office. The most frequently cited "beginning point" of the modern presidency is the administration of Franklin Roosevelt. In 1939 Congress passed legislation authorizing appointment of six administrative assistants in the White House Office and creating the Executive Office of the President, a more inclusive institution embracing the White House Office, the Bureau of the Budget, and some other supporting agencies. Since that time both the White House Office and the Executive Office of the President have grown inexorably. In 1937 there were 37 employees of the White House Office; by 1954 there were 266; and by 1971 there were some 600.[14] When the Executive Office of the President was created, it was made up of six agencies (four of which have since disappeared). By 1973 the Executive Office of the President included some 20 agencies. It embraced such important elements as the Office of Management and Budget (the successor to the Bureau of the Budget), the National Security Council, and the Council of Economic Advisors — and such specialized units as the Special Representative for Trade Negotiations and the Council on Physical Fitness. Agency personnel had long since spilled out of the White House proper and had filled the Old Executive Office Building (once sufficient to hold the State, War, and Navy Departments) next door, a New Executive Office Building on the north side of Pennsylvania Avenue, and numerous smaller buildings in the neighborhood of Lafayette Park across from the White House.

Even more important than a growth in size has been a change in the working relationships. During the Truman administration, the president would meet daily at 10 A.M. with a dozen staff members.[15] By the time of the Kennedy administration, staff members themselves were beginning to develop staffs of noticeable proportions. Theodore Sorensen, special counsel to the president, who was a prime coordinator for domestic policy, was assisted by Myer Feldman, Richard N. Goodwin, and Lee C. White. As we have already seen, the Johnson administration had 20 staffers, and the Nixon administration 28 working on domestic policy *alone*. This was a far remove from the White House staff member reporting directly to President Roosevelt or President Truman. Or take the seemingly small matter of lunching arrangements. As late as the Eisenhower administration, there was a single White House mess. Less important staff members often got to know the ranking members of the staff in relatively relaxed noon conversations. In the Johnson administration it was necessary to have two servings, and in the Nixon administration a second dining area was added. It was called the "Executive Dining Room," and was reserved for staff. Another opportunity for informal contacts and a wide acquaintance with colleagues had vanished.

Thomas E. Cronin, a leading student of presidential politics, tells us that by the late 1960s the White House staff had a rather marked differentiation.

> *The day of the "general purpose aide" with an entirely undefined portfolio seems a thing of the past for White House staff. To be sure, many of the White House jurisdictions are not rigidly prescribed, but those claiming to be generalists thrive not "at large," but in particular functional or substantive assignment areas, within, for example, public relations, foreign policy, or domestic program areas.*

Cronin further tells us that each of the functional groupings tends to recruit its own "types" — economists, defense intellectuals, political lawyers, or whatever — and that each group has a set of shared attitudes about the others with whom they are dealing. Although he is careful to specify that the White House staff could be further subdivided into more functional groupings, the five to which he calls attention are congressional relations, administrative and public relations, national security and foreign policy, budget and economic policy, and domestic policy and legislative program.[16] The first two of these White House groupings provide interface between the president and other elements of the Washington political environment, such as Congress and the press. Cronin's last three staff groups correspond directly to the policy areas we have discussed: national security and foreign policy to international involvement, budget and economic policy to economic management, and domestic policy and legislative program to the others.

If one turns from the White House Office to the larger Executive Office of the President, one can find further evidence of the effects of the policy areas on organizational structure. There are now so many agencies under this roof that one cannot classify all of them as falling into given policy areas, but one can make such statements about some of the most important components of the Executive Office. The National Security Council, the Central Intelligence Agency, and the Foreign Intelligence Advisory Board provide institutional support for international involvement. The Office of Management and Budget (although its mandate runs across the whole ambit of governmental activity) and the Council of Economic Advisors have certainly facilitated the tasks of economic management. As the seventies began, the only element needed to complete the symmetry of a differentiated White House staff with institutional support coming from a major Executive Office agency was a broadly conceived general-purpose unit articulating and coordinating domestic policy.

THE DOMESTIC COUNCIL

In April, 1969, President Nixon appointed a President's Advisory Council on Executive Organization, chaired by Roy L. Ash. The Ash Council began with a study of the Executive Office of the President and made recommendations on which the president acted in March, 1970. His Reorganization Plan No. 2 created a Domestic Council, and renamed the Bureau of the Budget as the Office of Management and Budget. The rationale for these moves was set forth in the message transmitting the Reorganization Plan to the Congress:

> *Essentially, the plan recognizes that two closely connected but basically separate functions both center in the President's office: policy determination and executive management. This involves 1) what the government should do, and 2) how it goes about doing it. My proposed reorganization creates a new entity to deal with each of these functions: It establishes a Domestic Council, to coordinate policy formulation in the domestic area. This cabinet group would be provided with an institutional staff, and to a considerable degree would be a domestic counterpart to the National Security Council. It establishes an Office of Management and Budget, which would be the President's principal arm for the exercise of his managerial functions. The Domestic Council will be primarily concerned with* what *we do; the Office of Management and Budget will be primarily concerned with* how *we do it, and* how well *we do it.*

A presidential reorganization plan takes effect unless Congress disapproves within a stated time period. There was insufficient congressional opposition to Reorganization Plan No. 2 for this to happen, and the new agencies came into being on July 1, 1970.

The original members of the Domestic Council were the president (as chairman); the vice president; the secretaries of the treasury, interior, agriculture,

commerce, labor, health, education and welfare, and housing and urban development; the attorney general; the postmaster general; and the director of the Office of
Economic Opportunity. These Council members were important in many ways.
Beyond whatever responsibilities they exercised as cabinet members, they chaired
Council committees, and the president relied on their political experience when
decisions were being made. When busy men are given new responsibilities, though,
it is well to inquire about the staff that is going to carry out these tasks. So it was in
this case. The mandate given the new Council was very broad. The president's
message said:

> *There does not now exist an organized institutionally staffed group charged*
> *with advising the President about the total range of domestic policy. The*
> *Domestic Council will fill that need. Under the President's direction, it will*
> *also be charged with integrating the various aspects of domestic policy into*
> *a consistent whole.*
>
> *Among the specific policy functions in which I intend the Domestic Council*
> *to take the lead are these:*
> *—Assessing national needs, collecting information and developing*
> *forecasts, for the purpose of defining national goals and objectives.*
> *—Identifying alternative ways of achieving these objectives, and recom-*
> *mending consistent, integrated sets of policy choices.*
> *—Providing rapid response to Presidential needs for policy advice on*
> *pressing domestic issues.*
> *—Coordinating the establishment of national priorities for the allocation*
> *of available resources.*
> *—Maintaining a continuous review of the conduct of on-going programs*
> *from a policy standpoint, and proposing reforms as needed.*

These responsibilities are not going to be discharged by already busy men.
This is apparent, not only from the scope of the mandate given to the Domestic
Council but also in the explicit references to an institutional staff that was to be
created. President Nixon appointed John D. Ehrlichman as the first executive
director of the Domestic Council, and Kenneth R. Cole, Jr., as deputy director. By
November, 1972, they had appointed six assistant directors, and, as indicated in
Figure 1–1 on page 14, all the assistant directors had appointed small staffs of their
own. Less formally, John Ehrlichman was the trusted aide of President Nixon and
the principal link between the president and the Council staff. Kenneth Cole was in
charge of the day-to-day operations of the Domestic Council, and each of the
assistant directors headed a "shop" in charge of some substantive area. These staff
personnel were, in a very real sense, the operating arm of the Domestic Council.

In the balance of this book we shall be concerned with the activities of the
Domestic Council staff as it was organized during the first 2½ years of its exis-

tence. (The information comes from interviews with staff members conducted from October 26, 1972, through December 1, 1972.[17] Consequently the pattern described is that developed from July, 1970, through December, 1972. The Domestic Council staff was reorganized as part of a general reduction in the size of the White House staff at the beginning of President Nixon's second term.) These activities were not new to the White House. As we have already seen, almost the same number of aides were involved in quite similar doings in the Johnson administration.[18] But we can learn how Richard Nixon organized his staff to suit his working habits and to be able to operate in the power situation in which he found himself. The Domestic Council was the principal locus of domestic decision-making. Hence knowing about it reveals some not unimportant information about the way the Nixon White House operated.

The Nixon White House, of course, was no less differentiated than any other modern executive establishment, and it is well to be explicit about what this study does *not* tell us. We do not learn about foreign policy, save for the fact that the problems were so pervasive as to affect domestic policy. We see congressional relations and party politics only tangentially, as there were separate staffs with principal responsibilities for these matters. The whole public relations apparatus is missing from our purview, and we do not know who, if anyone, was supposed to provide the "sustained, second-level advocacy" Daniel P. Moynihan said was so important if Nixon proposals were to be accepted. And since those involved in the Watergate affair were located elsewhere in the Nixon White House,[19] a study of the Domestic Council casts little light on that episode.

On the other hand, we can address questions that go beyond the Nixon administration, in the sense that they deal with continuing problems of the presidency. What kinds of persons were appointed to these staff positions? What kinds of skills did they bring to their tasks? What kinds of interpersonal ties linked them together as a group? How did they perceive the attitudes of the voters to be in the various areas of public policy, and what did they understand the preferences of the president to be on the same matters? How did they serve as mediators between the president and the many other persons in the complex political environment? All of these topics, as we have been arguing in this chapter, shape the behavior of an administration. If we can trace some of their effects during the 1970–72 period, we can gain not only some understanding of the activities of the Nixon administration but also some appreciation of the presidency itself.

SUMMARY

The behavior of an administration results from the interaction of some seven factors: the character and work habits of the president, the power situation outside the White House, the attitudes of persons appointed to responsible positions, the attitudes of the voters as expressed in the most recent election, the policy areas with which the administration must deal, the complexity of the political environment, and the constraints set by the political calendar. The first four factors are relatively fluid and produce differences from one administration to the next. The last three are relatively stable and account for the constancies that may be observed in succeeding administrations. The slowly changing considerations (the attitudes of the voters, the policy areas, and the complexity of the environment) are those most likely to result in institutional change, and the direction of institutional change has been in the direction of a differentiated presidency. Separate units have developed in the White House to provide interface with related actors (Congress, the press corps, and so forth) and to deal with major policy areas, national security, economic management, and domestic policy. This book will examine the staff dealing with domestic policy, the Domestic Council, as that group operated during Nixon's first term.

NOTES

[1]James David Barber, *The Presidential Character: Predicting Performance in the White House* (Englewood Cliffs, N.J.: Prentice-Hall, 1972).

[2]Charles O. Jones, *The Minority Party in Congress* (Boston: Little-Brown, 1970), Chapter 2. The term "power situation" is used by Professor Barber to speak of the amount of support or opposition a president can expect.

[3]The phrase is Douglass Cater's. See *The Fourth Branch of Government* (Boston: Houghton Mifflin, 1959).

[4]The six policy areas to be discussed in the following pages were discerned in an analysis of the State of the Union Messages delivered by Presidents Truman, Eisenhower, Kennedy, and Johnson. For evidence supporting the generalizations I shall offer, see John H. Kessel, "The Parameters of Presidential Politics," *Social Science Quarterly*, June 1974, pp. 8–24. For more basic work, and a showing that quite similar policy areas apply to Congress, see Aage R. Clausen, *How Congressmen Decide: A Policy Focus* (New York: St. Martin's Press, 1973).

[5]The United States is obligated by treaty to support countries in many parts of the world. Consider what would happen if some disastrous chain of events should require that we send troops to all those countries simultaneously.

[6]Interest groups were not included in the earlier definition of "power situation" because they do not tend to be for one president and against another so much as they are consistently for their own interests.

[7]Legislation providing for a legislative budget (which passed Congress in 1974) requires presidents to submit preliminary budget data in November. This will alter the annual pattern a bit.

[8]This eight-year pattern has been suggested by Richard E. Neustadt. For his interpretation, see *Presidential Power with an Afterword on JFK* (New York: Wiley, 1968), pp. 198–199.

[9]"How Ford Runs the White House," *U.S. News and World Report*, September 23, 1974, p. 32.

[10]On this, see William J. Daniels and James E. Underwood, "Program Innovation and Program Output in New York State: The Role of Governor Rockefeller," a paper prepared for delivery at the 1972 Annual Meeting of the American Political Science Association; for Mr. Rockefeller's own views, see "Address of Gov. Nelson A. Rockefeller at the 1973 Annual Meeting of the American Political Science Association," (New York: Third Century Corporation, n.d.).

[11]I am indebted to Thomas E. Cronin for this information on the way the Johnson White House was organized in 1967.

[12]Thomas E. Cronin, "Everybody Believes in Democracy Until He Gets to the White House," *Law and Contemporary Problems*, Summer, 1970, p. 593.

[13]Thomas E. Cronin, "The Textbook Presidency and Political Science," a paper prepared for delivery at the 1970 Annual Meeting of the American Political Science Association, Los Angeles, California, September 7–12, 1970, p. 39.

[14]Alex B. Lacy, Jr., "The Development of the White House Office, 1939–1967," a paper prepared for delivery to the 1967 Meeting of the American Political Science Association, Chicago, Illinois, September 5–9, 1967; Thomas E. Cronin, "The Swelling of the Presidency," *Saturday Review of the Society*, February, 1973, pp. 30–36.

[15]John Hersey, "Ten O'Clock Meeting," reprinted in Nelson W. Polsby, ed., *The Modern Presidency* (New York: Random House, 1973), pp. 57–69.

[16]Thomas E. Cronin, "Everybody Believes in Democracy Until . . .", pp. 593–603.

[17]I had interviews with 16 staff members and shorter telephone interviews with four more staff members. See Appendix B for the interview schedule.

[18]Hubert Humphrey had called for the creation of a "National Domestic Policy Council" in Los Angeles on July 11, 1968.

[19]The only exceptions to this appear to be John Ehrlichman, to the extent that he was involved as a senior political advisor of the president, and Mr. Ehrlichman and Egil Krogh because of their involvement in the "Plumbers" operation. It happens that I did not interview either man.

Chapter 2

A Group Perspective

The marching orders for the Domestic Council came from the Oval Office. Leaders[1] used almost identical wording to say this. Ted Weber[2] commented simply:

Well, the president decides what the Domestic Council is to do . . .

Bart Compton was only slightly more expansive:

The president basically decides what we should do. He identifies issues he wants to decide after staff action. More of the action takes place in areas he's interested in.

Kenneth Cole modified this to the extent of drawing a distinction between assignments given to the Council and the internal operations of the Council staff:

The president decides what the Domestic Council should do, and I decide how it will get done.

Not everyone who was asked for his overall impression of how the Council worked identified it simply as a presidential agency. A number of persons compared the Domestic Council with other units in the Executive Office of the President. A rather common description of the Domestic Council was that it served as a "domestic" National Security Council. Tom Parsons put it in these words:

When the president came into office in '68, there was on the foreign policy and defense side a pretty well structured organization for policy development in the White House, that is, the National Security Council. But on the domestic side, where there are probably more players and a greater variety

25

of problems, there was not a structured policy development organization. And it's always been my view that was our role. It seems that it works pretty much in parallel with the NSC with Kissinger on the one side and Ehrlichman on the other side.

Frank Miller contrasted the Domestic Council with the Office of Management and Budget by suggesting that the Council's attention was more narrowly focused:

We watch out for the things the president has told us to watch out for, and they (OMB) watch out for the whole government.

These statements about presidential interest and comparisons with other important policy units certainly are consistent with the kinds of issues the Domestic Council was considering. Indeed, the general areas in which the Council staff was active — busing, the environment, health, crime and drugs, energy, tax policy, welfare reform, revenue-sharing, and so forth — almost constitute a catalogue of the issues that required sensitive handling in the early seventies.

What did the Council staff do in these policy areas? There was no single pattern. At some times action had to be taken quickly, and the "process" was oral communication pure and simple. At others, detailed studies were made and submitted for presidential decision. A frequently followed sequence was that staff members were given directions by the president, they got into contact with other persons in the bureaucracy and the wider environment, and then they reported back to the president with information and recommendations on the subject. Ralph Schmidt spoke about this process:

A typical, if any problem is typical, matter may be that the president has expressed interest in a particular problem, and a committee of the Domestic Council itself will be created with one of the cabinet officers in charge of a working group, and that working group will put together papers. Depending on the scope of the process, that may go on for a period of time, then gradually be brought up again to the principals' level, and ultimately, perhaps, an option paper will go to the president. The Domestic Council staff, so to speak, in all of this, certainly is a back-up. In many cases, we do not do all the detailed work so much as we act as a catalyst, raise questions, and, to the extent that there's a need for some additional type of expertise, we may bring in someone from the outside also.

Since responsibilities assigned to the Domestic Council called upon them to receive initial instructions from the president, confer extensively with others, and ultimately report back to him, it follows that they frequently saw themselves in an intermediary role between the president and other political actors. Mary Hickman spoke at some length about two closely related tasks growing out of this linking role between the president and the departments and agencies:

> *First, there is a coordinative function to make sure his general policy standards and policy directions are carried out in the most general sense. I've never been very happy with labels like conservative and liberal, but if the president says, "The federal government is too large; the budget can't stand it, and the people want it cut," then I want it cut. If he says, "I want government restructured so as to bring power to a lower level," and these are the general directions that he's given, then certainly the Domestic Council has a requirement to make sure that these (instructions) are carried out, that they are translated from the general to the particular. In addition, our other major function is to put out the major fires, the controversies between cabinet officers that they don't resolve. The president obviously hasn't got time to get into every single debate on every programmatic responsibility or to referee which department has jurisdiction in a particular case or to translate the major decisions of the bureaucracy into a public decision. So it's really two things. One is to translate from the general to the particular on the way down; the other is to put out the fires on the way back up.*

As Fred Winters described the jobs he had to do, he saw them coming both from the president and the wide constituency to which the president was responsible:

> *The work assignments are generally administered through John Ehrlichman and generally come from the president. That is a major source, whether it be an initiative or we have a problem in this area or a phone call. Would you put something together on it? Or it may be different in terms of a final work product. It may be a memo to the president or it may be a piece of legislation or it may be just generally put out a fire in a particular area, either in an agency or in the countryside, so to speak. The other way that it comes is kind of up the chain, and that's from our own contacts both within the government and around the country. You know, we get some phone calls saying the potential is here for some serious problems and you ought to know about it. So that generates work going up, and we'll go across the street (to the White House) saying here's the problem, and we'll then get in contact with the Labor Department saying this, that, and the other thing. So generally the work assignments come from those two sources.*

Members of the Council staff were the president's men operating in a political environment. They carried messages about the president's wishes in one direction; they picked up information that ought to be brought back to the president and his senior advisers. In order to work effectively in this linking role, they had to develop means of maintaining communications on both sides. They were working in the Executive Office Building because someone trusted them, but to do their job they had to develop relationships of confidence with others.

Scott Manning mentioned some of the work habits that had been developed:

> *I was talking to one of the departments the other day, and said that probably one of the reasons why the Domestic Council functions effectively is that many of us are lawyers, and are prepared to present an issue in an entirely balanced way. . . . When I came down here, I was informed that all the White House staff was nothing but a bunch of ideological eunuchs, that they had no point of view, but that seems to me our most effective function. We don't have an ax to grind with anybody, and we don't weight the evidence.*

Obviously, Manning went on to explain, it was impossible to take a completely neutral position because one's own selection process inescapably weighed the evidence to some extent. Yet, in his feeling, he had touched upon the essentials of the best style for Domestic Council staff members. They were operating in a highly political atmosphere, and they did so as agents of the president. That they wore presidential livery was at once a source of great power and great suspicion. They could exercise the power most effectively if they could abate the suspicion. And to do that, they not only had to deal candidly and faithfully with others, but contrive ways to let the others discern that the dealings were entirely honorable.

But this gets ahead of our story. In Chapter 4, we shall return to the tasks assigned to the Domestic Council. In order to understand how they handled these responsibilities, we need first to examine the staff as a group, and then take a careful look at the environment in which they carried on their work. When I use the word *group* I mean something more than a number of people. To be considered as a group, rather than a simple collection of individuals, the members must share attitudes with one another, and there must be a reasonably stabilized pattern of interaction between the members.[3] Furthermore, by taking the group as the focus of this study, we imply that we are not interested in the activity of individuals except as it affected the behavior of the group, and that our interest in more inclusive organizational units (the Executive Office of the President, the executive branch, and so forth) lies in how the larger units constrained and delimited the activities of the Domestic Council staff. In other words, we shall be considering aggregative properties from the individual level, integral properties (such as the size and activities of the Council staff) and structural properties (such as patterns of communication and influence) from the group level, and contextual properties derived from the more inclusive political environment in which the Council staff was situated.[4] In this chapter we shall see how the staff members were recruited, what skills they brought to the Council, what attitudes they had concerning public policy, the degree to which they shared those attitudes with each other, what communication pattern existed between the staff members, and how they influenced each other.

RECRUITMENT AND QUALIFICATIONS

The Domestic Council staff was not recruited in any systematic way. Most of the ranking members of the staff had been advance men (those charged with arriving in a community several days in advance of a candidate's appearance and making the necessary arrangements) or had held related positions concerned with campaign scheduling in 1968. This category included John Ehrlichman, Kenneth Cole, and three of the assistant directors. Others came to their positions in a variety of ways. A few had held other White House positions and had joined the Domestic Council staff when it was first organized. Several had worked for other government agencies, had come to know Domestic Council personnel in this way, and had been invited to join the staff when there was a vacancy. Some had known other staff members previously, in law school for instance, and had been contacted by their friends. One person was hired because John Ehrlichman had asked Stanford Law School (where he had gone) to make a recommendation. Still another had come to Washington to be interviewed for a position with another agency, had been told that the Domestic Council was looking for persons, and had come for an interview. This pattern was anything but an exhaustive search, but it was resulted in a job offer. It was not dissimilar from that followed in previous administrations. Alex Lacy, who has studied White House Office staffs from 1939 through 1967, tells us that about two-thirds of Eisenhower's initial staff had been active in the 1952 campaign, and about half of those who came to the White House with John F. Kennedy had been involved in the 1960 campaign. For the rest, it was a matter of "chance, circumstance, and a good bit of luck."[5] White House recruiting patterns are much closer to the casual, who-do-you-know-and-are-you-free-when-staff-is-being-hired manner in which staffs are assembled on Capitol Hill than they are to the recruiting patterns of major corporations.

The Domestic Council staff members were much younger and better educated than their White House predecessors. Their average age was 35, and if one excludes John Ehrlichman and two others who had passed their fortieth birthdays, the average age drops to 32. The mean age of White House staff members for each of the four preceding administrations had been 45. Of 21 Domestic Council staff members,[6] twelve had law degrees, seven had Ph.D. degrees, and the other two had degrees in business administration. The proportions of those holding law degrees in the Kennedy, Johnson, and Nixon administrations were 43 percent, 35 percent, and 57 percent, respectively, and the proportions of those with Ph.D.'s were 14 percent, 7 percent, and 33 percent.

One simple way of thinking of the men and women who came to the

Domestic Council staff is to divide them into rough categories of advance men and
"seeded players." The important thing about the advance men was not that they
had been involved in the Nixon campaign in a particular capacity, but that they had
worked with the president over a period of time and had been able to establish
relationships of trust and confidence with him.[7] One who had not been an advance
man explained it this way:

> *One thing you must be able to do is understand what the president wants. In
> that regard, you really only get good communication with the president if
> you're performing very well —and to perform very well, you've got to have
> good communication. So the key is the guy who's running the Domestic
> Council. If he's got the president's confidence, and the president has a good
> working relationship with him, the Council can be potent and effective
> because it will have this communication. Without it, I think you might as
> well take the Domestic Council out of the White House, because its real
> strength is that it does have this relationship. It can bring the president's
> vantage point to bear on problems, and it brings certain concerns of the
> president to bear which are different than OMB and different than an
> agency.*

By "seeded players" I mean those whose early attainments suggest that life
will deal kindly with them. Leafing through résumés, one encounters "the Louis
Brownlow prize for the best article on public administration," "Phi Beta Kappa,
University of Michigan, London School of Economics, and Harvard Law School,"
"high school student cabinet president, class valedictorian, all-state election in
three sports, and Outstanding School Citizen for the state," "Yale University and
magna cum laude from Columbia Law School," and "MIT with a double major
in chemical engineering and humanities and Harvard Law School." Too much
should not be read into these background qualifications. Similar characteristics
could be found among the assistant professors at a state university or the junior
members in a good law firm. In common with other well-educated young persons,
they are open to new ideas and able to analyze complex matters, but still a little
short on experience. What does count is that the advance men and the others they
recruited brought a mix of identification with the president and capacity to acquire
expertise. As we shall see, identification and expertise turn out to be keys to
influence within this White House group.

ATTITUDES ABOUT POLICY

When we turn to questions of public policy, we need to avoid the twin delusions that
those on the Council staff were either ignorant or omniscient. A much better way to
view the cognitive abilities of policy-makers is to use Heinz Eulau and Kenneth
Prewitt's concept of a policy map. As they explain it:

> *Policy map-making need not be a conscious intellectual process; and, for this reason, the analogy between the policy-maker's mental mapping of the environment and the geographer's mapping of the territory should not be pushed too far. However, the analogy is suggestive: even if policy-mapping is not a conscious process, it is not altogether arbitrary and random. The bits and pieces of information that come to the policy-maker's attention, the demands that are made on him or that he makes on himself, and the expectations that he entertains about the future provide a more or less accurate guide of what is possible or desirable in the making of public policy.* [8]

The policy-maker's cognitive map is not complete, any more than a map is identical with the terrain it represents, but it provides an adequate guide to the issues with which he must deal. In the case of intelligent persons who are on top of the issues in their charge (as with the Domestic Council staff members), the policy maps include considerable detail.

Our measures of the policy maps of the Domestic Council staff members focus on the half dozen policy areas discussed in the preceding chapter: international involvement, economic management, social benefits, civil liberties, natural resources, and agriculture. [9] The mean attitudes of the staff members are displayed in Figure 2–1. There are sufficient differences from one policy area to another that any general characterization of these White House staff members as liberal or conservative, as usually willing to use government power or usually reluctant to do so, would be quite misleading. Ranked in terms of willingness to regulate or spend, the areas are natural resources, international involvement, social benefits, civil liberties, agriculture, and economic management. This ordering corresponds to observable tendencies in administration policy. The Nixon administration was most activist in the area of natural resources (the president devoted much of his 1970 State of the Union message to environmental problems, and he created a vigorous Environmental Protection Agency); was next most likely to use American power and resources in the international arena (the president often spoke of his hope for a generation of peace, and he was willing to travel widely in a search for international agreements); followed a moderately conservative policy with respect to social benefits, civil liberties, and agriculture; and was least likely to sanction government activity in the economic area (the president waited until it appeared that no other technique would work before invoking price and wage controls in 1971, and he vetoed any number of bills to hold down spending). Hence, our confidence in the measures in Figure 2–1 rests not only on their basis in the policy areas but in their ability to capture the central thrusts of administration activity.

The next question is the extent to which those policy scores represent agreement among staff members. A score of 4.0 would suggest a moderate policy, but an average of 4.0 could come about in any number of ways. Half of the people could have scores of 7 (maximum use of government power) while the other half had scores of 1 (minimum use of government power). Alternatively, everyone might have an individual score of 4. Both circumstances would result in a mean

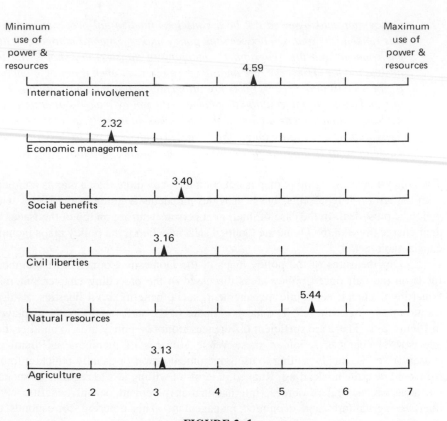

FIGURE 2–1

Policy Attitudes of Staff Members

score of 4.0, but would represent radically different circumstances. Both the possibility of agreement and the interpersonal dynamics would be affected in important ways. Newcomb, Turner, and Converse have explained why shared attitudes are so important to the existence of a true group:

> *To the degree that members have similar attitudes that they express to one another, they come to share those attitudes. When such sharing represents acceptance of group-relevant rules, group norms exist. . . . The general consequence of a relatively high degree of sharing any attitude among group members are that individuals' attitudes are supported, and that attraction among the sharers is increased; as a consequence . . . individuals internalize the rules so that they become self-enforcing; thus one member becomes substitutable for another, or for the group as a whole.*[10]

Consequently it behooves us to look for evidence of consensus.[11]

Inspection of our data reveals that a consensus did exist on these issues. The extent of the consensus, however, also varied from policy area to policy area. That can be shown in two ways. First, we can compare the standard deviations of the attitudes of staff members with those of the American public.[12] The average standard deviation from the mean attitudes of staff members was 1.29; the average standard deviation for the general public was 1.82. If anything, these average standard deviations understate the difference between the Domestic Council staff and the general public. Five of the ten staff standard deviations fell between .8 and 1.2; seven of the ten standard deviations for the public fell between 1.8 and 2.2. In other words, the range of staff opinion (about the means reported in Figure 2–1) tended toward ±1, while the range of public opinion tended toward ±2. The group attitudes were likely to be concentrated among three of the seven magnitudes on the scale, while most of the public attitudes were distributed across five of the seven magnitudes. This comparison enables us to infer a staff consensus because of the relatively restricted variation in their attitudes.

It is also possible to compute a measure of consensus. The figures for this consensus measure for each policy item are given in Table 2–1.[13] Since a value of +1.0 means complete agreement on the policy (within the limits of our ability to

TABLE 2-1
Staff Consensus on Policy Issues

Issue	*C**	*Issue*	*C*
Cut government spending	.89	Guarantee farm income	.67
Control pollution	.78	Increase police authority	.50
Racial busing	.78	Help pay medical bills	.44
Military spending	.67	Increase welfare payments	.33
Use economic controls	.67	Foreign aid	.33

*Higher scores indicate greater agreement. For details on the consensus measure, see Appendix A2.3.

measure that agreement), and a value of 0 indicates that there is an equal distribution of views, it can be seen that consensus does exist. The extent of agreement, however, varies from item to item. When the particular issues are combined by policy area, the values are: economic management, .78; natural resources, .78; agriculture, .67; civil liberties, .62; international involvement, .50; and social benefits, .39. While there was consensus among staff members on all these policy matters, there was the greatest agreement on economic matters, on which the Republican party has traditionally been united, and the least agreement on matters of foreign policy and social welfare, which often divide the party.

Having seen that consensus existed for the group as a whole, we ask next whether most staff members contributed to that agreement. (It is possible that some staff members did not share their colleagues' views on policy matters.) To ascertain this, we shall use a measure of attitudinal proximity.[14] This takes on a value of +1.0 if there is complete agreement, and a value of 0 if there is complete disagreement. When these scores were calculated between each staff member and the group median, the highest proximity score was .93 and the lowest was .62. Eleven of these 16 proximity scores were between .80 and .89. No person, in other words, was exactly at the group median (the dominant position in the group), but neither did the attitudes of any group member place him very far away.

The structure of interpersonal proximity on these policy attitudes (in Table 2–2) reveals this consensus also extends to pairs of individuals. The highest proximity score for any dyad is .97; the lowest is .68. Three persons—Mark Jensen, Frank Miller, and Ted Weber—are a little more distant from their colleagues than the other 13 members. The principal finding, however, is that 74 of the 120 pairs have proximity scores between .80 and .89. This level of interpersonal agreement does not represent unanimity, but neither does it suggest anything approaching disagree-

TABLE 2-2
Matrix of Interpersonal Proximity on Policy Attitudes

	B	C	D	F	G	H	J	L	M	N	P	R	S	T	W
Archer	.95	.90	.88	.85	.82	.89	.74	.81	.72	.88	.82	.87	.85	.92	.74
Bailey		.88	.88	.88	.82	.89	.71	.83	.70	.85	.88	.89	.82	.81	.79
Compton			.89	.89	.81	.90	.83	.87	.76	.92	.87	.85	.87	.96	.78
Daniels				.87	.87	.88	.72	.93	.71	.87	.83	.85	.83	.90	.87
Flint					.87	.85	.81	.82	.85	.87	.95	.85	.87	.88	.87
Gruber						.85	.83	.85	.82	.92	.87	.82	.97	.85	.72
Hampton							.76	.83	.79	.90	.82	.74	.93	.92	.76
Jensen								.76	.72	.87	.81	.68	.83	.79	.70
Leggett									72	.88	.82	.81	.88	.90	.82
Miller										.79	.82	.78	.82	.78	.68
Norris											.87	.82	.92	.90	.75
Phillips												.82	.87	.87	.87
Redman													.85	.87	.75
Schmidt														.88	.75
Tuttle															.76
Weber															

Higher scores indicate greater agreement. For details on proximity measure, see Appendix A2.4.

ment over the thrust of public policy. The agreement already noted on the group level extended to the individual members of the group as well.

One final check on all these conclusions ought to be reported. It is conceivable that the individual attitudes were mediated by organizational assignments in such a way that the data we have reviewed have been misleading. The problem is that we have measured staff members' attitudes in all six policy areas, even though most Domestic Council staff members worked in strictly delimited substantive areas. Ralph Schmidt raised this objection directly:

> *Some of those are areas that are not only not in my area of responsibility, but I'm virtually ignorant as to them. They refer to administration views that I don't need to know.*

To check on the possibility that the views of all staff members might not be representative of those who had responsibilities in given substantive areas, the entire analysis — attitudes, consensus, and proximity — was repeated for just those staff members who were directly concerned with each policy area. The results varied in some details, but did not alter our understanding of their shared attitudes in any major way.

This distribution of attitudes suggests a lively exploration of a relatively restricted range of alternatives. So far as their recommendations were a product of their own views,[15] the existing consensus reduced the probability that some alternatives were very actively considered. Since most favored government action to control pollution, it is unlikely that there was serious advocacy of a laissez faire posture in this policy area. Similarly, shared attitudes about the desirability of cutting government spending made it improbable that there was a vigorous search for ways to increase the proportion of the gross national product devoted to the public sector.

At the same time, the concentration of attitudes in a restricted range tended to produce a lively discussion and considerable exchange of information among policy-makers.[16] Essentially, the argument is this. If there is complete agreement, nothing can be said that will provide any new information. If there is complete disagreement, if one policy-maker believes in a guaranteed income for farmers and another feels farmers should not receive any government support whatsoever, nothing that either could say would be persuasive to the other. But when there is consensus—incomplete agreement—there are enough shared premises to permit easy communication, and there is enough diversity of view to allow each person to augment the others' information. Since one of the major responsibilities of the Domestic Council is to gather information about policy alternatives, it is important to understand how their attitudinal consensus facilitated this essential communication.

THE COMMUNICATION PATTERN

In order to deal with communication directly, it is necessary to know just a bit about how such networks can be analyzed. An example of a simple communication network is given in Figure 2–2. The arrow diagram (technically, a directed graph) at the top of the page tells us that Angus can send messages to Bruce, Bruce can

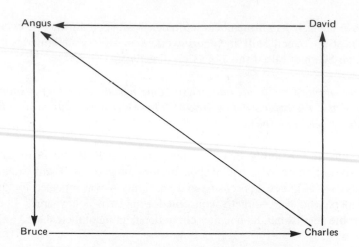

One-Stage Communication Matrix

	Angus	Bruce	Charles	David
Angus	0	1	0	0
Bruce	0	0	1	0
Charles	1	0	0	1
David	1	0	0	0

Two-Stage Communication Matrix

	Angus	Bruce	Charles	David
Angus	0	0	1	0
Bruce	1	0	0	1
Charles	1	1	0	0
David	0	1	0	0

FIGURE 2–2

Simple Communication Network

send messages to Charles, Charles can send messages to both David and Angus, and David can send messages to Angus. This same information is conveyed in the one-stage communication matrix. Here, *1* indicates the presence of a communication channel, and *0* indicates its absence. Hence the *1* in Angus's row and Bruce's column has the same meaning as the arrow running from Angus to Bruce in the diagram above. If one takes the row sums, he learns the number of messages that a person can send, and if he takes the column sums, he learns the number of messages that can be received. The row sums tell us that Charles can send two messages, and that Angus can receive two messages. The two-stage communication matrix (obtained by squaring the one-stage matrix) informs us about the messages that can be sent in two stages. For example, Angus can send a message to Charles through Bruce. Therefore there is a *1* in the (Angus, Charles) cell in the top row of the two-stage matrix. The diagrams are easier to read if there are a limited number of persons involved in a communication network, but the matrices are easier to read if a large number of persons make the arrow diagrams too dense. The matrices also give the relative importance of any person more swiftly (through the row sums and column sums), and are more useful if one wishes to examine two-stage or three-stage communications whose matrices may be obtained by taking the square or the cube of the original matrix.

We are now ready to examine the pattern of interaction within the group. Table 2–3 gives the one-stage communication matrix for 19 Domestic Council staff members.[17] There are two clear characteristics to this communication matrix. First, there was a tendency to communicate to others within the same "shop." These communication links — which can be discerned in the *1*'s lying on either side of the main diagonal — are hardly surprising. The staff members were working on closely related matters, and their offices were often in close proximity. However, this

TABLE 2-3
Communication Matrix for Domestic Council Staff

	A	B	C	D	Fl	Fr	Fu	Ge	Gr	H	J	L	M	N	P	R	S	T	W
Archer	–	1	0	0	0	0	0	0	1	0	0	0	0	0	0	0	0	0	0
Bailey	1	–	0	1	1	1	0	0	1	0	0	0	0	0	0	0	0	0	0
Compton	0	0	–	0	0	0	0	0	0	0	0	0	0	0	0	0	0	0	0
Daniels	0	0	0	–	1	1	1	1	0	0	0	0	0	0	0	0	1	0	0
Flint	0	0	0	0	–	0	0	0	1	0	0	0	0	0	0	0	0	0	0
Frederick	1	0	0	1	1	–	0	0	1	0	0	0	0	0	0	0	0	0	0
Fuller	0	0	0	1	0	1	–	1	0	0	0	0	0	0	0	0	0	0	0
Gearhart	0	0	0	0	1	0	0	–	1	0	0	0	0	0	0	0	0	0	0
Gruber	1	0	0	0	1	0	0	0	–	1	1	1	0	0	1	0	1	0	0
Hampton	0	0	0	0	0	0	0	0	1	–	0	0	0	0	0	0	0	0	0
Jensen	0	0	0	0	1	0	0	0	1	0	–	1	1	0	0	0	0	0	0
Leggett	0	0	0	0	0	0	0	0	1	0	1	–	1	0	0	0	0	0	0
Miller	0	0	0	0	0	0	0	0	0	0	1	1	–	0	0	0	0	0	0
Norris	0	0	0	0	1	0	0	0	1	0	0	0	0	–	1	0	0	0	0
Phillips	0	0	0	0	0	0	0	0	1	0	0	0	0	0	–	0	0	0	0
Redman	0	0	0	0	0	0	0	0	0	0	0	0	0	1	1	–	0	0	0
Schmidt	0	0	0	0	0	0	0	0	1	0	0	0	0	0	0	0	–	0	0
Tuttle	0	0	0	0	1	0	0	0	1	0	0	0	0	0	0	0	0	–	0
Weber	0	0	0	0	0	0	0	0	0	0	0	0	0	0	0	0	0	0	–

This matrix is for one-stage communication. Row entries denote channels through which messages are sent; column entries denote channels through which messages are received.

intra-shop linkage was incomplete. There were only two shops in which each person mentioned all his colleagues.

The second characteristic — a tendency to send messages upward — was much stronger. Whenever there is a column containing several *1*'s, the chances are quite good that the person to which the column refers was a formally designated leader. The leaders were nominated both by their own aides and by other leaders. The communication network that held the staff together was distinctly hierarchical. The leaders were simultaneously in touch with their own aides and with each other.[18]

A few more messages were being originated by aides than by leaders, and many more communications were being received by leaders than by aides. The average number of links through which leaders sent messages was 2.5; the average number of links through which aides sent messages was 2.9. However, the mean number of paths through which leaders received communications was 5.2, while the mean number of paths through which the aides received communications was only 1.2. It was the leaders who occupied the central positions in this communication network.

Much more can be understood by examining the indirect communication that was revealed in the two-stage matrix. The number of communication paths goes up exponentially; there were only 49 one-stage links, but there were 168 two-stage links in this communication network. Hence the one-stage links only begin to tell you about the nature of the communication that went on within the group. One matter that the squared matrix brings to light is some activity on the part of aides that helped knit the staff together. As one aide explained:

> *The assistant directors on the Domestic Council staff see each other on a regular basis. People that are below that level have more contact with people that are below that level than they do with the assistant directors themselves. If a problem comes along in a particular substantive area, I'd think of someone on the Domestic Council staff. If it's something in agriculture, I'd call Norm McCullough. If it's something in transportation, I'd call Nancy Schuster. And so forth. That would be my first reaction. You'd call someone on the Domestic Council staff, and then go on from there. And there is a tendency to start with someone on your own level. I'd always start with someone working in a shop before I'd call an assistant director.*

Much of this contact between aides in different shops was carried on by aides in one shop responsible for "long-range plans." The line between "long-range plans" and the responsibilities of others was vague at best. Consequently, there was a fair amount of contact between aides in this shop and others with parallel assignments. Many of the two-stage channels that held the staff together as a group were created in this way.

The stronger pattern in the two-stage matrix, however, is once more the importance of hierarchy. Again, aides were at the origin of a few more communication channels than the leaders. The average aide was at the beginning of 10.1 two-stage communication paths,[19] while the average leader was at the beginning of 9.5 two-stage paths. There was, however, a dramatic difference in the number of ways communications were received. The mean number of two-stage channels through which leaders received messages was 18.5, and the mean number of two-stage channels through which the aides received messages was only 2.5. This gives the distinct impression of reports flowing upward through a number of channels, then laterally in a relatively intense communication network among the leaders, and instructions flowing back down to aides through very few channels. The aides, after all, needed the attention of their superiors if they were going to be effective. Ward Norris spoke quite directly about this:

> *What I try to do is to develop policy that can be sold to Phillips, and if he buys it, sold to Ehrlichman as administration policy.*

The leaders had the power.

THE PATTERN OF POWER

Power is a subtle matter. It is delicate to exercise, and difficult to measure. Yet it is central to any political group, so we must grapple with some of its complexities. Two aspects of power are particularly important to our understanding: the structure of power, and the means of exercising power.

Students of power have distinguished at least four means through which one person may influence another: legitimacy, identification, expertise, and sanctions.[20] Legitimacy rests on the belief that one ought to be obeyed because he has been duly elected or appointed to office and therefore has a generally accepted right to issue orders to others. Identification refers to the respect a person has for another who is a member of the same group and who has been working to attain common ends. The power of expertise depends on a feeling of confidence a person has in one who possesses special knowledge about a subject (such as a doctor or a lawyer) or who has demonstrated that he is unusually well informed. Sanctions, of course, refer to rewards and punishments.

Influence networks may be analyzed in much the same fashion as communication networks.[21] Figure 2–3 presents an example with four persons: Jim, the boss; Karl, a relatively new person hired for specific technical skills; Lance, a long-time employee; and Mike, another employee, who has worked for Jim for a shorter period. The arrow diagram at the top of the page suggests the influence relationships between them. Karl, Lance, and Mike all respect Jim's legitimacy. Lance is concerned about sanctions Jim can exercise, and identifies with him. Mike is also aware of the possibility of Jim's sanctions. Karl and Mike both identify with Lance,

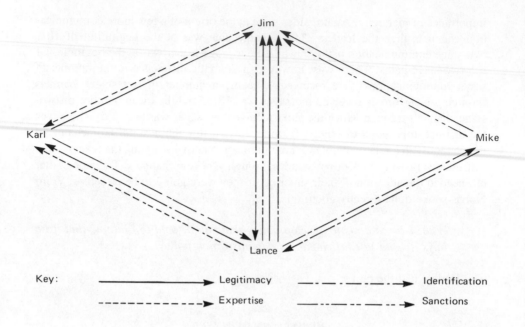

FIGURE 2-3

Sample Influence Network

who in turn identifies with them. Jim and Lance both respect Karl's expertise. The number of these influence relationships means the arrow diagram is a little more difficult to read than one for a communication matrix. With different kinds of lines used to denote the different types of influence relationships, the resulting arrow diagram is denser and requires a little more scrutiny before it can be understood. Information about the number of influence relationships is conveyed in the one-stage influence matrix immediately below the arrow diagram.[22] The *1* in Jim's row and Karl's column means that Jim is subject to Karl's influence in one way (expertise), and the *1* in Jim's row and Lance's column means that Jim is subject to Lance's influence in one way (identification). The *3* in Lance's row and Jim's column means that Lance is subject to three influence relationships from Jim (legitimacy, identification, and sanctions). Therefore if one takes the row sums, he can learn the number of ways a person is subject to influence, and if he takes the column sums, he can learn the number of ways a person can exert influence.

As with the communication matrix, a two-stage matrix can be determined by taking the square of the one-stage matrix. The two-stage influence relationships, however, are a little more complex than the two-stage communication paths. For one thing, the nature of the influence may change. There are two-stage influence relationships in which only one means of influence is involved; for example, from Karl to Mike because Lance identifies with Karl and Mike identifies with Lance. But there are also two two-stage influence relationships from Karl to Mike through Jim. Jim is influenced because of Karl's expertise, and Mike is influenced by Jim by means of sanctions and legitimacy. Hence there is one expertise-sanctions path, and there is another expertise-legitimacy path. This particular example also points up the possibility of two-stage feedback relationships. Consider the relationships between Jim and Lance. Jim identifies with Lance, and Lance is influenced by Jim through identification, legitimacy, and sanctions. Now what happens if one tries out an idea on the other? If Jim asks Lance, the merit of Lance's answer is going to be underscored by Jim's identification with Lance; if Lance asks Jim, Jim's answer will be amplified by three means of influence. The two-stage influence relationships therefore have the potential of strong reinforcement. If two group members agree with each other on the merits of a question, and feedback influence relationships exist between them, very powerful forces (either from within the group or elsewhere in their environment) will be needed to dissuade them. Here we see the roots of group inertia.

Table 2–4 presents data on the one-stage influence relationships within the Domestic Council staff.[23] The row sums tell us that aides were subject to a few more influence ties than were leaders, although those differences were not great. The column sums tell us there was a marked discrepancy in the number of ways the leaders and the aides could exercise influence. The average column sum for a leader was 13, while the average column sum for an aide was less than 1.

The two-stage influence relationships are more interesting, because they are far from obvious. First of all, the leaders exerted almost every bit of two-stage power. The aides had some one-stage influence, but in almost every case it was "dead end": The person being influenced by an aide was not in a position to influence anyone else. In fact, only one aide exercised *any* two-stage influence.

TABLE 2–4
Influence Matrix for Domestic Council Staff

	A	B	C	D	F	G	H	J	L	M	N	P	R	S	T	W
Archer	–	0	0	0	0	2	0	0	1	0	0	0	0	0	0	0
Bailey	2	–	0	0	0	2	0	0	0	0	0	0	0	0	0	0
Compton	0	1	–	0	1	1	0	0	0	0	0	0	0	0	0	1
Daniels	0	0	0	–	3	2	0	0	0	0	0	0	0	0	0	0
Flint	0	0	0	0	–	1	0	0	1	0	0	0	0	0	0	0
Gruber	1	0	0	0	1	–	1	1	1	0	0	1	0	1	0	0
Hampton	0	0	0	0	1	4	–	1	0	0	0	0	0	1	0	0
Jensen	1	0	0	0	0	4	0	–	3	0	0	0	0	0	0	0
Leggett	3	0	0	0	0	3	0	0	–	0	0	0	0	1	0	0
Miller	1	0	0	0	0	2	1	1	1	–	0	0	0	0	0	0
Norris	0	0	0	0	1	2	0	0	1	0	–	2	0	0	0	0
Phillips	1	0	0	0	0	3	0	0	1	0	0	–	0	0	0	0
Redman	0	0	0	2	2	3	1	0	0	1	1	2	–	1	0	0
Schmidt	1	1	0	0	0	2	0	0	0	0	0	0	0	–	0	0
Tuttle	1	0	0	0	0	4	0	0	0	0	0	0	0	0	–	0
Weber	0	0	0	0	1	2	0	1	0	0	0	0	0	1	0	–

This matrix is for one-stage influence relationships. Row entries denote the number of ways a person is subject to influence; column entries denote the number of ways a person is able to exert influence.

Second, some of the two-stage influence relationships were not apparent to the staff members themselves. For example, Dan Bailey mentioned Stuart Leggett as a person he barely knew:

> *I have no dealing with Stuart Leggett. I don't think I've met him more than twice, so I just have no direct feeling for the whole range of problems that he has responsibility for or his staff guys.*

Yet Bailey was subject to four two-stage influence ties from Leggett.

Third, the leaders were subject to quite a few reciprocal influence relationships. The average number of such feedback relationships for the leaders was 5.3. And, as we saw in our examination of the sample influence network, such reciprocal relationships exercise a strong reinforcing effect. If the persons taking part in such relationships are in agreement to begin with, these feedback ties can make a group quite rigid. Our examination of the attitudinal consensus earlier in this chapter revealed the staff members were not in complete agreement, but a consensus existed that made it likely that there would be a detailed exchange of information within a relatively restricted range of alternatives. Here we see the interpersonal network that anchored that consensus. These two things, a consensus on the desirability of given courses of action and a network of influence between group leaders, made it likely that the group would opt for "satisficing" proposals, that is, proposals to which no group leader objected.[24] There have been many comments to the effect that "wrong" decisions have been made in the White House because White House staff members are isolated from those elsewhere in Washington who presumably could explain the error of their ways. At least as it applies to the Domestic Council staff, this explanation is wrong. As we shall see in the next chapter, the staff was anything but isolated from the political environment. To the extent that they persisted in courses of action, the explanation is to be found in their attitudinal consensus and in the reciprocal relationships of influence between leaders (and, of course, the wishes of the president). They were convinced of the propriety of the policies they proposed, and if any leader had doubts, he could be reassured by one of his peers.

Another important conclusion emerges when we take a separate look at each of the means of exercising influence. In general, the informal interpersonal relationships tended to support the formal hierarchical relationships. That is, identification and sanctions were generally associated with legitimacy. Aides respected their leaders, and were concerned about their possible opposition. To a degree this was also true of expertise. A number of comments suggested aides were impressed with the information possessed by the directors. Bill Hunter said:

> *John Ehrlichman to me is the renaissance man of the Domestic Council. He continually amazes me by how he's able to be on top of a whole range of domestic problems.*

Mark Jensen remarked that in his opinion:

> *Ken Cole is clearly the best informed. He's the focal point for all the information on the Council.*

Yet expertise was unique among the means of internal influence in that it was the only way one could go outside the formal channels of authority. The central power on the Council staff was held by the former advance men, who had the trust of the president. But in every case in which a relative newcomer was able to establish an independent reputation, and in every case in which a leader was able to become influential outside his own shop, the reason was that others were convinced that he knew what he was talking about. The internal importance of expertise was stressed in comments such as these:

> *The staff members are all fully informed. If they weren't, they wouldn't be there.*

> *I think this place sorts out pretty much on the basis of proven competence and knowledge of problems.*

In the next chapter we shall see one reason information was such a potent internal lever — the complexity of the political environment with which these staffers had to deal.

SUMMARY

In this chapter we have reviewed the group life of the staff members who handled domestic problems on behalf of President Nixon. The original leaders of the group had been chosen by the president on the basis of relationships of trust developed during the 1968 campaign and during the early months of the Nixon administration. These former advance men had selected others they trusted in the unsystematic manner that typifies White House recruiting. As a group, they were most disposed to use government power and/or resources on matters of natural resources and international involvement, preferred moderately conservative policies in social benefits, civil liberties, and agriculture, and were opposed to government spending and regulation of the economy. There was a consensus among group members on these policy preferences, but the extent of the consensus varied according to the policy in question. The interpersonal relationships among staff members tended to support the formal hierarchical relationships. That was true both of communications, in which the leaders received more messages, and of influence, in which the leaders had many more means by which they could exercise power. Taken together, the attitudinal consensus and reciprocal relations of influence between the leaders stabilized the group and gave it a vitality above and beyond any organization charts that might be used to describe it.

NOTES

[1]The word *leaders* will be used to refer to the executive director, deputy director, and assistant directors. All others, namely, those who work in the assistant directors' shops, will be called *aides*.

[2]In almost all cases pseudonyms will be used for staff members. The only exceptions will be references to the leadership provided by John Ehrlichman or Kenneth Cole, and an occasional statement by Kenneth Cole about the work of the Council. In most cases the names of agencies mentioned by staff members will also be changed. If, for example, the original statement mentioned the Labor Department (or the secretary of labor), the quote I give in the book may refer to the Commerce Department.

[3]This definition of group is essentially that used by David B. Truman. See *The Governmental Process* (New York: Knopf, 1951), Chapter 2. For a review of the voluminous group literature, see the chapters by Kelley and Thibaut, and Collins and Raven in Gardner Lindzey and Elliott Aronson, eds., *Handbook of Social Psychology*, 2nd ed. (Reading, Mass.: Addison-Wesley, 1969), vol. 4, pp. 1–204.

[4]For a fine discussion of the levels-of-analysis problem, see Heinz Eulau and Kenneth Prewitt, *Labyrinths of Democracy* (Indianapolis: Bobbs-Merrill, 1973), Chapter 2.

[5]Alex B. Lacy, Jr., "The Development of the White House Office, 1939–1967." The data on age and education in the succeeding paragraph also come from Lacy's paper. Note that the figures are not quite comparable. Nixon data refer to the Domestic Council staff, while those for earlier administrations refer to the White House Office.

[6]The number of staff members referred to will vary a bit, depending on the number for whom particular data are available.

[7]This, of course, is an ancient theme. The very names of early officials, chamberlain and chancellor, imply access to the king and his bedchamber. See T. S. Tout, *The English Civil Service in the Fourteenth Century* (Manchester, England: The University Press, 1916).

[8]*Labyrinths of Democracy*, p. 520.

[9]See Appendix A2.1 for a description of these measures.

[10]Theodore M. Newcomb, Ralph H. Turner, and Philip E. Converse, *Social Psychology: The Study of Human Interaction* (New York: Holt, Rinehart and Winston, 1965), p. 255.

[11]Strictly speaking, we cannot show the existence of sharing, as that requires both consensus and knowledge of the consensus acquired through interpersonal communication. The existence of consensus and the pattern of communication (to be shown later in the chapter) make it very likely that sharing exists.

[12]For a discussion of this use of standard deviations, see Appendix A2.2.

[13]For a description of this measure of consensus, see Appendix A2.3.

[14]For a description of the proximity measure, see Appendix A2.4.

[15]This is a most important qualification. Staff members are charged with reporting the reactions to proposed policies of as wide a range of people as possible.

[16]On this, see R. Duncan Luce, "The Theory of Selective Information and Some of its Behavioral Applications," in R. D. Luce, ed., *Developments in Mathematical Psychology* (Glencoe, Ill.: The Free Press. 1960). p. 39, and John H. Kessel, George F. Cole, and Robert G. Seddig, eds., *Micropolitics: Individual and Group Level Concepts* (New York: Holt, Rinehart & Winston, 1970), pp. 461–462.

[17]For information on the data that were used to establish the existence of these communication links, see Appendix A2.5.

[18]Some isolated individuals also appear in the matrix. They were either very junior aides or persons whose contacts were largely external. Sometimes the isolation is only apparent; some of the staff members are linked to others who were not interviewed and who consequently are not included in this matrix.

[19]An example of a two-stage communication path, as the reader may recall from Figure 2–2, would be between Angus and Charles in which Angus gives a message to Bruce, who in turn tells Charles.

[20]Herbert A. Simon, Donald W. Smithburg, and Victor A. Thompson, *Public Administration* (New York: Knopf, 1950), pp. 188–201. See also Dorwin Cartwright, "Influence, Leadership, Control," in James C. March, ed., *Handbook of Organizations* (Chicago: Rand-McNally, 1965), Chapter 1.

[21]For similar analyses, see Arthur L. Stinchcombe, "On the Use of Matrix Algebra in the Analysis of Formal Organizations," in Amitai Etzioni, ed., *Complex Organizations* (New York: Holt, Rinehart & Winston, 1961), pp. 478–484, and John G. Kemeny and J. Laurie Snell, *Mathematical Models in the Social Sciences* (Boston: Ginn, 1962), Chapter 8.

[22]There is loss of information here in moving from the graph form to the matrix form; specifically, one does not know from this matrix how the influence is being exercised. Furthermore, in order to use a *1* for each type of influence relationship, one must be willing to assume they are all equally important. Otherwise, some type of weighting must be used.

[23]For discussion of the data on influence, see Appendix A2.6.

[24]This is not quite what Herbert Simon meant by a "satisficing" proposal. Strictly speaking, it is the selection of a behavior alternative whose consequences are deemed acceptable by the group members from among the set of alternatives that are perceived. Here I have limited the "right to object" to group leaders because the leaders exercised all the power within the group. On Simon's concept, see his "A Behavioral Model of Rational Choice," in *Models of Man* (New York: Wiley, 1957).

Chapter 3

The Political View
from the White House

No political group exists in a vacuum, least of all one located in the White House. Demands, importunings, and stimuli to action bombard aides of our chief executive. At the same time political opposition, institutional resistance, and constitutional limitations remind them of things they may not do. It has long been a commonplace that a group's understanding of their environment helps to distinguish between politically viable courses of action and those that are only theoretically possible. But we are just beginning to understand the extent to which and the ways in which a group's environment shapes its internal organization.

In their pioneering Bay Area study, Heinz Eulau and Kenneth Prewitt interpreted a group's decision structure and social organization as "collective adaptation to the need for becoming a decision-making group that can govern as well as adaptation to the challenges presented by the common tasks of governing."[1] Furthermore, they found that an intricate environment has profound effects on a political group that must cope with it.

> *It would seem that in primarily responding to internal complexity in its social relations, governing style, and governing practices, the council is in fact responding, if only indirectly, to the complexity of its human environment. The larger the city and all that size implies—complexity, heterogeneity, social pluralism, and so on—the more likely it is that the council will turn inward and develop a configuration of social relations, governing styles, and practices that is conducive to its internal adaptation, its ability to jell as a group and get along, in the face of what may well be experienced as a complex and puzzling environment.*[2]

It is altogether likely that this line of reasoning applies to the Domestic Council staff. In the first chapter we began to appreciate something of the complexity of the political environment by reviewing the number of persons and groups involved in the discussion of a single issue, and by projecting this against the number of issues with which the White House had to deal in each of half a dozen policy areas. In the last chapter we saw that the staff members were generally agreed with each other on the extent to which government power and resources should be used, and the policy areas in which government activity was desirable. We also saw the communication and influence patterns that enabled the staff "to jell as a group and get along in the face of . . . a complex and puzzling environment." In this chapter we want to scrutinize the composition of the political environment in a good deal more detail. Specifically, we need to better understand the Domestic Council staff's perception of and relationships with the president, voters, cabinet members, congressional leaders, interest group spokesmen, bureau chiefs, and Republican party leaders. We shall begin this by asking how the staff members saw the tasks before them.

PERCEPTION OF A COMPLEX ENVIRONMENT

In order to find out what was on the White House agenda, staff members were asked what they thought were the most important problems confronting the administration. Their immediate answers—such as, "You got the rest of the afternoon?"—indicated that the White House had to contend simultaneously with a broad range of matters. Some of the staff members spoke directly about substantive matters, and most who replied in this vein began by excluding nondomestic topics:

> *First, to obtain a settlement on Vietnam. That, of course, isn't the business of the Domestic Council.*

Not surprisingly, many of the problems mentioned were those that had occupied a fair amount of attention from the Domestic Council. Carl Baker said:

> *In terms of specific programs, I think a good deal on the domestic side is in terms of taxes, the fiscal problems of tax reform. That's just a very important problem area. And in addition to that, we have all the carryover, so to speak. The welfare problem, the problem of increasing the quality and availability of health care, and so forth.*

Bruce Frederick's list began with energy, but he went on to mention several other matters:

> *I think energy is a very important problem. The overall problem of a national growth policy may be so broad as to be unanswerable, but we've got to keep that in mind. We've made some errors in the past that have led to the problems that the cities are now experiencing. You know, the decreasing*

> *tax base as the richer people move to the suburbs, urban decay and that whole range of problems. The still unresolved problem of racial justice in this country. The perception of many people that government is impinging too much on their lives. Of course, your civil liberties. The welfare situation. These seem to me to be the highlights. There are a hell of a lot of other problems, but these are the biggest ones.*

The list of substantive problems was long, but welfare reform, housing, mass transit, health care, and other urban problems were among the most frequently cited by these White House aides.

Another view called attention to the organizational problems that inhibited governmental response to either presidential wishes or particular substantive problems. Mary Hickman put it quite simply:

> *The bigness of government and the ineptness of government.*

Stuart Leggett was a bit more expansive:

> *First of all, the desirability and the need to somehow get a better handle on the governmental apparatus, the bureaucracy or whatever you want to call it, which to some extent may be an organizational kind of problem. That permeates policy-making and development at all levels. You can have the best program in the world, and it can still die down in the trenches if they're not carrying it out. Another area, a broad area of concern, is the area of making government more effective. Much of the decision-making process could be placed at different levels, at state and local levels, that is now focused here in Washington.*

This view of organization as the most important problem is related to Nixon administration emphasis on such matters as government reorganization and revenue sharing. The slow pace of action on these items, though, called attention to another challenge in the political environment, dealing with Congress and public opinion. Reflecting on the lack of congressional response during the first administration, and looking forward to the second Nixon administration, Alan Hampton said:

> *We've got to learn how to work with Congress in order to advance the president's programs. The new Congress certainly isn't going to be more sympathetic, and perhaps less so. Another problem, although this may not be so serious, is we've got to get people to believe we're serious about the programs we're putting forward.*

Pat Thornburg explicitly linked congressional responsiveness to the amount of support that could be elicited from the public.

I don't think —and I understand there's criticism to the contrary —that we have failed to present domestic policy direction and a full scale of domestic programs. I think our problem is in being able to convince the Congress to at least take a crack at doing it the way we have suggested or at least close to it. Or in having the nation comprehend what we're trying to do as a worthwhile change, or a modification of existing circumstances. It just took one devil of a long time to get revenue-sharing through against a lot of very strong opposition —which finally caved because there was a lot of pressure built up popularly. . . . I sometimes get the feeling that the nation as a whole says, ok, we elected you. Now run the country and make it happen. . . . Or they say, gee, that sounds like a terrific idea. It's time to change welfare around. They don't perceive that they've got to put some pressure on the congressmen, who are not about to jump until they feel that pressure. But dealing with the Congress that is composed of the opposite political party makes it our most difficult political problem.

The difficulties in dealing with an opposition Congress were compounded by the fact that the Nixon administration was guided by a desire to reduce the level of government activity wherever possible. Since many Democrats did not share these views, the Nixon administration faced principled as well as partisan opposition. If Nixonian principles were to be implemented, a great deal of work was going to have to be done to translate the abstract ideas into viable programs. Ward Norris pointed this out:

The most important problem is to make the president's philosophy consistent on the operating level. The president has an insight on something —to reduce the level of governmental expenditures, and the federal government role. . . . But to get this philosophy consistent on the operating level, it's necessary to work out on a program-by-program basis just what needs to be done, and then work actively to induce the private sector to take over the delivery of some of these social services.

Fred Winters spoke about the lack of maneuvering room available to the Nixon administration because of the legislation placed on the books by preceding administrations.

Well, I think it's clearly how to develop within his philosophy a progressive yet relatively conservative approach to domestic problems. It's going to be tough, because we came in at a time when we're saddled very heavily with both the successes and the failures of the Great Society years. Unfortunately, both Congress and the public have a very hard time discriminating between what has been successful and what has not been successful. And, as you know, there's not room in the present budget for new initiatives. So the only place you can get that is by taking what are clearly unsuccessful programs, or programs where we're just not getting our dollars' worth, and dismantling them some way. Then we can use those resources, usually applied to the same problem, hopefully in a different way, to increase our output to the problem. We've got to be careful that we don't heighten expectations that we're going to have a miracle in four years. We'll do well if we get a solid foundation laid. I think the president has the kind of stability and patience to do it this way.

The president. He, after all, was the key to all the hopes and plans of the White House staff. If the long list of domestic problems was to be attended to, if governmental institutions were to respond in a different way, if a new tone was to be sounded, the president had to do it. It was quite in keeping with his central role that Scott Manning spoke directly about the need for leadership from him:

The most crucial need right now is for the president to exert positive leadership in putting the country back together. The tensions generated by racial problems and the war have created serious tensions on the whole fabric of society. What is needed is a clear view of the emerging needs of society. The president has an unusual and uncanny skill at feeling the currents of American public opinion. The trick is to stay just far enough ahead of developing opinion, and to exert a pragmatic style of leadership. In this way, he can hold the country together as it passes through a cathartic period of reassessment.

While the character of these problems was affected by the political circumstances of the time, the number of problems was not unique to the Nixon administration. Every recent administration has had to contend with an increasing list of challenges. Yet it was not the number of problems that best characterized the White House's political environment; it was the *interrelatedness* of those problems. This point was not made by any staff member. They focused on specific aspects of their environment. But they were not talking about separable things. If a program was to be brought to bear on a substantive matter, organizational problems were going to have to be solved. If the government was going to be reorganized to deliver services more efficiently, Congress had to be persuaded. If an opposition Congress was to agree to executive reorganization, citizens were going to have to understand the need for it and persuade their representatives. If the president was to have a plausible case when he appealed for public support, specific proposals and arguments to support them were going to have to be developed by the staff. And so on.

Opportunities were inherent in this political environment no less than constraints. The key to both lay in the mutual dependence of the elements we have been examining. It was difficult to achieve any end before related problems had been attended to; but, by the same token, success in any one area made it easier to achieve further success in a related matter. It took a certain combination of wit and character to see that. Intelligence was needed to grasp the related nature of the problems, and staff members had to have the kinds of personalities that predisposed them to react positively to challenges if they were to take advantage of the situation. Nevertheless, the potential for success in one area that leads to further accomplishment in another, and the possibility of continuing frustration, were both inherent in the interrelated political environment.

Another striking feature of the context in which the Domestic Council staff conducted its business was the number of other persons who had to be consulted: experts whose advice was needed, spokesmen whose constituencies were concerned with White House actions, leaders whose positions entitled them to deference, and scores of others. When the political landscape was crowded with actors seeking attention, it was patent that everyone could not be recognized at once. Therefore, staff members had to develop some ways of sorting out these persons, of determining whose views were of vital import and whose views were of lesser consequence.

The mean staff rankings of the importance of the several actors with whom they had necessary business (presented in Figure 3–1) reveal a distinct pattern.[3] The president was clearly Number One. Indeed, there was as much distance between the chief executive and the next most important group, the voters, as there was between the voters and the least important inhabitants of the White House political environment. Aside from the president, those involved were split into two fairly distinct categories. Voters (always in mind if not physically present), cabinet members, colleagues on the Domestic Council staff, and congressional leaders were seen as the more important grouping. Interest group spokesmen, bureau chiefs (that is, ranking civil servants), and Republican party leaders were less important in this White House perspective. The first group could be said to exert a more general influence, the second to be listened to in special circumstances. Indeed, the particular influence of congressional leaders (their counsel carries most weight on legislative matters in the domain of their own committees) may well account for their ranking between those with general and those with specialized influence. This is a possibility we should keep in mind as we review the staff members' perceptions of those with whom they came in contact.

THE PRESIDENT

The Domestic Council staff did not see the president's attitudes as differing in any fundamental way with their own.[4] The mean perceptions of Mr. Nixon's policy views, shown in Figure 3–2, suggest the same general ordering to the use of government power and resources as we saw when we looked at the staff attitudes: a predisposition to employ governmental influence with respect to natural resources and international matters, a "go slow" policy concerning agriculture, social benefits, and civil liberties, and a genuine reluctance to affect the economy through

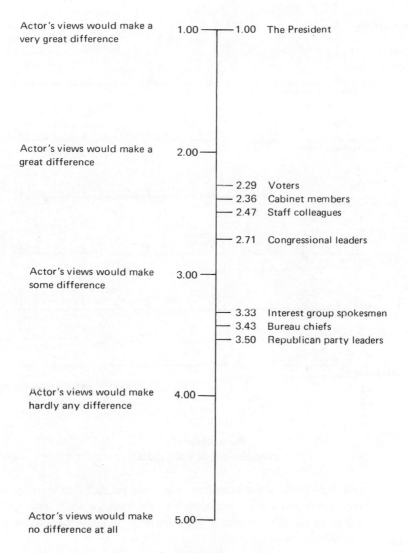

FIGURE 3–1

**Relative Importance of Actors
in Domestic Council Environment**

controls or new spending programs. A comparison of the mean scores within each policy area shows that President Nixon was seen as slightly more willing than the staff to use power and resources in international matters and to support agricultural income, and a shade less willing to do so with respect to economic management and social benefits. The staff attitudes on natural resources and civil liberties were

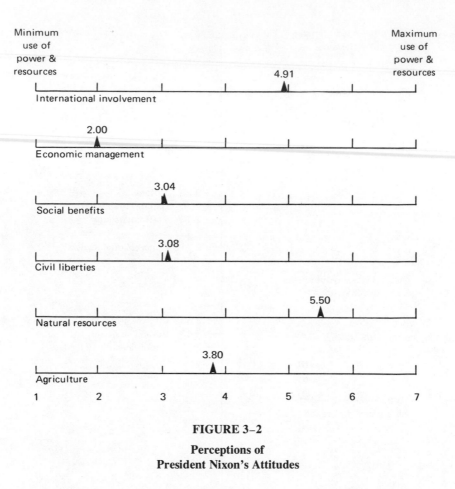

FIGURE 3–2

**Perceptions of
President Nixon's Attitudes**

indistinguishable from those of the president. The same relationship between staff attitudes and their perceptions of the president's views emerges when the comparison is confined to those staff members spending a substantial amount of time working in the policy areas in question.[5]

A more important comparison deals with consensus.[6] Staff members were more likely to agree with each other on where Mr. Nixon stood than they were to agree with each other on the same issues. The data on this are presented in Table 3–1. A high value (1.00) indicates complete agreement, and a low value (.00) indicates that the answers are distributed evenly among all response categories. With the exception of agriculture (the policy area to which the least amount of staff time was devoted), the consensus figures increase as one moves from the staff members to their perception of the president to the specialists' perception of the president. This means that the consensus that existed among staff members about the president's views was equal to or greater than the consensus that existed on their

TABLE 3-1
A Comparison of Agreement among Staff Members

Issue area	Consensus*		
	Among staff members	On perception of president	On perception of president by specialists
Economic management	.78	.89	.92
Social benefits	.39	.38	.64
Civil liberties	.62	.76	1.00
Natural resources	.78	.78	1.00
Agriculture	.67	.38	.50

*For a description of the measure of consensus used, see Appendix A3.3.

own policy views. And in every case there was greater agreement about the president's preferences among those concerned with the policy area than there was for the staff as a whole. They agreed on what the president's positions were.

Positive knowledge of Nixonian positions was vital for many reasons. To begin with, the president's views stipulated the bounds within which staff activity was carried forward. Two aides commented on this:

He sort of defines my subject, I wouldn't be working on something if he didn't think it was important.

The president's views make all the difference in the world. You know, I don't mean to sound like I'm marching off a cliff when I say that, but if he says, this is it . . .

If he says, this is it. Here Tom Parsons began to hint at some of the nuances of the relationships between the president and the staff members who were working for him. David Archer, one of the leaders who had built up a good working relationship with the president, provided more detail in speaking about what he would do if he found himself in disagreement with Mr. Nixon:

I would argue the point unless I knew that the point had been argued before and lost —and then I'd do what I'm told. In other words, if he has a difference of opinion from what I think we should do, I'll have a mechanism through John Ehrlichman to make that known to him. Or, if John thinks it important enough, I'll see him directly on it. However, because John deals with him every day, and we don't because of our special areas of responsibility, five or six times out of ten, John will know the answer to how he feels about it and I won't. . . . But there's no question about it. If I know directly

*that he feels contrary to what I do, and I know he's focused on the problem
and knows he feels differently, we'll do it his way. He got elected, not us.*

These presidential aides knew when a determination had been made, and
they knew what the determination had been. Consequently, they had a better conception of what courses of action were possible and what had been ruled out. This
positive knowledge of presidential intent is important. One argument for policy
coordination in the White House is that it provides a chance for presidential preferences to guide policy decisions. The difficulty this poses for those elsewhere in
government is that they don't know whether aides are speaking for the president or
simply invoking their own preferences. The evidence we have just reviewed indicates that Domestic Council staff members did know where the president stood, and
that when novel questions came along, communication channels were available
through which authoritative answers could be obtained.

VOTERS

Perception of the voters' preferences is a more complex matter. The president takes
specific positions on public policy matters, and members of the White House staff
receive a steady stream of cues about those positions. Voters, on the other hand, are
distributed along a continuum. Some favor more action on the part of the government; some prefer less. And the flow of information about voters' attitudes is
intermittent at best. Fortunately, we do have some data that cast light on this
process.[7] Preliminary data from a study of public attitudes conducted at the same
time make it possible to compare the staff perceptions of public attitudes[8] with the
positions taken by the voters themselves. The comparison reveals that the staff
perception of public views was generally accurate, but that it was biased in the
direction of less use of government authority and resources. Both of these aspects
require some scrutiny, so we shall look at both of them in turn.

In order for staff members to perceive a position that can be attributed to
"American voters," there must first be a measure of agreement among the public.
Perceptual accuracy in this case will depend on two things: the existence of a
consensus, and the ability of the observers to apprehend the location of that consensus. Table 3–2 presents data on both these points. The left-hand column gives
information on the extent of consensus among the public.[9] The right-hand column
gives information about the extent to which the staff apprehended that consensus.[10]
If the two figures are the same, the meaning is that the staff understood the location
of whatever consensus existed. Table 3–2 indicates that there was a public consensus on most issues at the time of the 1972 election, and that the Domestic Council
staff members were aware of the location of that consensus in seven of ten cases. In
two of the remaining cases, the staff mode was one magnitude lower than the
voters' mode. Staff members slightly underestimated the extent to which voters said

TABLE 3-2
Comparison of Public Consensus on Policy Issues with
Staff Perception of that Consensus

Issue	Consensus Among General Public*	Staff Perception of Consensus**
Control pollution	.81	.81
Military spending	.60	.35
Cut government spending	.54	.54
Increase police authority	.46	.06
Racial busing	.43	.43
Guarantee farm income	.40	−.25
Foreign aid	.20	.20
Increase welfare payments	.17	.17
Help pay medical bills	.15	.15
Use economic controls	−.05	−.05

*For information on this measure, see Appendix A3.6.
**For information on this measure, see Appendix A3.7.

they were willing to increase police authority and to spend for military purposes. Only on agriculture was the staff badly in error. These data support an overall conclusion that the staff perception of voters' attitudes was generally accurate.

Another way of judging perceptual accuracy is to compare the mean figures for staff perceptions with the mean positions taken by the voters. This leads to slightly different conclusions (in part because the mode, used as the basis of the consensus measure, and the mean reflect different properties of the distribution). We can see this in Figure 3–3, in which the mean staff perceptions are compared with the mean positions taken by Nixon and McGovern voters. The general conclusion that staff perception was accurate is still valid, particularly if comparison is made with Nixon voters. Only in agriculture was the staff perception as much as a single magnitude away from the preferences of the voters who put them in office. But we also see clear evidence of a specific perceptual bias. There is an interesting contrast between Nixon and McGovern voters on foreign and domestic matters. Nixon voters were more predisposed to use American power and resources in international affairs, whereas McGovern voters were more likely to use governmental authority and funds on domestic policies. Yet regardless of whether the Nixon voters or the McGovern voters took the more "conservative" position on a given policy, Domestic Council staff members judged the voters to be still less willing to employ the power and resources of the federal government.

We know that the electorate is an important element in the White House political environment; yet here we have clear evidence that there was a systematic misperception of the voters' preferences. Why? Our data do not permit us to explore this question in detail, but the evidence suggests that the staff members did not

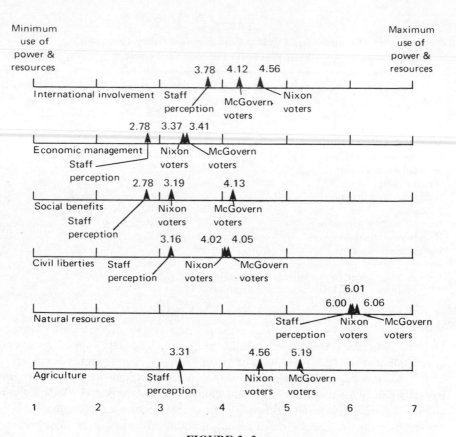

FIGURE 3–3

**Comparison of Staff Perceptions
of Voters' Attitudes with Mean
Positions of Nixon and McGovern Voters**

focus on the voters' opinions, and in the absence of accurate information there was
some tendency to project their own attitudes onto the electorate.[11] How this happened can best be understood by inspecting the data in Table 3–3. The top line
shows the relationships indicated in Figure 3–3; the staff perceptions of voters'
preferences were biased away from governmental activity. The middle line shows
the extent to which staff members attributed their own attitudes to the public. This
happened a little less than half the time, and did not introduce any bias in either
direction. Staff members were equally prone to say that voters preferred more
government activity or less government activity than they did themselves. (In fact,
there was a wide spread in these judgments. There were a few cases where staff
members supported policies they thought the voters strongly opposed, and a few
cases where they strongly opposed policies they believed the voters supported.) The

TABLE 3–3
Comparison of Staff Attitudes and Voters' Attitudes

	Proportion of Attitudes (percentages add across)		
	Less willing to use govt. pwr./resources	*Identical*	*More willing to use govt. pwr./resources*
Staff perception as compared to voter attitudes	60.6%	20.6%	18.6%
Staff perception of voters as compared to staff attitudes	28.2	44.1	27.6
Staff attitudes as compared to voter attitudes	59.7	24.5	15.8

bottom line holds the key. The staff members themselves were less fond of using government power and resources than the voters, and, because their own attitudes provided the central tendency for their perceptions of the voters, a systematic bias in perception resulted.[12]

Another important point is that while voters in the abstract were thought to be quite important, Domestic Council staff members did not have that much contact with living, breathing voters. Ralph Schmidt voiced a typical complaint about the intensity of interest group activity as contrasted with the difficulty of finding out about voters:

> *There are five or six different consumers' groups that have different philosophical views about how our programs should be conducted. There are hundreds of lobbyists. I see them. Have I ever seen a housewife? Yes, but it's hard to find them because they don't come to town. I think that's the most honest way to answer your question. It's hard to find out what people are thinking because the only people that are represented in this town are the people that can afford to be represented. And that's bad.*

Mary Hickman also spoke about the lack of representation of voters, but she drew a slightly different conclusion:

> *There is no representative of the voters. We are, in effect, while we're here.*

It was not so much that cues from the electorate were being missed. Rather, there were relatively few cues about voters' preferences in an environment that was loaded with other cues.

Another point made by several staff members concerned the voters' low information level about the details of policy. From this they drew distinctions about occasions when voters' attitudes would and would not be important. One typical remark was:

> *In terms of a basic policy, public reaction would make a great deal of difference. In terms of a particular means of carrying out a basic policy, it would be less consequential.*

In other words, staff assessments of voters' preferences were not based on constant information or on a feeling that they must respond to public opinion at all times. The disposition of the voters was only one of several cues to which the staff had to react, and they were more likely to be responsive when the electorate was seen to prefer a basic policy direction rather than a specific means of executing that policy.

CABINET MEMBERS

The relationship between the Domestic Council staff and cabinet members was concerned with the specifics of policy determination. Most policy proposals were, in fact, hammered out in White House-department interaction. The relationship was also delicate. Whenever there was a difference of opinion about the wisdom of different courses of action, there was a real possibility of role conflict for both actors. As operating heads of executive agencies, the cabinet and subcabinet members had an interest in seeing the adoption of their department's proposals as administration policy. As presidential appointees, however, the department heads could be expected to keep their agencies in line with presidential wishes. The Domestic Council staff members had a delicate problem with deference. The cabinet member outranked the Domestic Council staff member,[13] yet the staff member was ultimately responsible to the president, who had appointed the cabinet member. In fact, the relationships were structured to minimize role conflict. The views of the cabinet members and the Domestic Council staff members both went to the president. The opinions of the cabinet members were always transmitted in unvarnished form, and the Domestic Council staff members could also add their own recommendations. This enabled the cabinet member to carry out his responsibility for advocating the views of his agency, and the Domestic Council staff member to do his job of making recommendations based on information assembled from a wide variety of sources. Not unimportantly, this arrangement also protected the president's interest in having a maximum amount of information in hand when he made his own decisions.

When a department made a determination about its policy preference, one method of obtaining White House support was a direct approach through the

Domestic Council staff. Ward Norris commented about the desirability of working through "normal channels" in this way.

> *First of all, we're likely to know that the department has made that determination, more likely by direct communication from the assistant secretary. If the secretary is involved, he may also contact us. We also keep a liaison with the Office of Management and Budget, through the budget review process, which is going on now. We have some indications as we sit in those meetings, you know, we have some ideas from that process. I think the normal approach, and the wise approach, is a very direct approach, in terms of making views known.*

While coming into the White House through the Domestic Council staff, and thence to the president through John Ehrlichman, had the advantages of speed and maximizing the information in the hands of those charged with policy coordination, this was by no means the only route cabinet members could use to reach the chief executive. Ted Weber listed several communication paths a cabinet member could use:

> *A cabinet member makes his views known through the working group immediately; he makes his views known through the cabinet meeting immediately; he makes his views known by a direct memorandum to the president. If there is any other vehicle he wants to use, he has that available to him as well. He can write a memorandum to John Ehrlichman, or he can write a memorandum to Cap Weinberger if it's a budget matter. If he finds, or he feels, he wants to make an additional argument to the president, he can go directly to the president.*

Even so, the bulk of department-White House business was not transacted by means of personal contact between the secretary and the president. There were simply too many messages between the bureaucracy and the Executive Mansion for any but the most important to be handled at the top level. Kevin Daniels pointed out some organizational consequences of the volume of communications:

> *Clearly, the big gun is that the secretary weighs in with the president. However, as in any organizational conduct of affairs, that's the big gun and that's reserved. So the next one is that the secretary talks to Ehrlichman and that puts it in at the top level, or the secretary or assistant secretary talks to OMB. Another level is the White House or Domestic Council staff level. That's usually the assistant secretary talking to me or to my opposite number in OMB. That's the traditional way to do it.*

Often departmental initiatives came from offices far below that of the sec-

retary. It was not unusual for those to be tested out at a subordinate level on the
Domestic Council staff at a preliminary stage in policy development:

> *The best way is for them to go up through their channels to their cabinet
> officer, and make their position known in that way, although that often isn't
> the case. There are other ways. One that comes to mind was something that
> the Labor Department wanted to do, and they called me and asked me. In
> effect, they lobbied with me. They said, here's what we're thinking about
> doing, and what do you think about it? Obviously, they were taking the
> approach of coming to me at my level to see if they could get me persuaded
> so I could go up this side to get that position or that policy accepted . . .*

It was frequently possible for departments to be persuasive with the White
House without any direct contact on their part. One reason lay in the sources of
information available to the departments. In the summer the Domestic Council staff
sought out ideas to identify major themes in coming presidential programs. They
turned to the agencies for information, and this had obvious consequences for policy
development. Pat Thornburg mentioned this:

> *We need OMB and departmental input in order to make decisions. We're
> not independent. Facts, after all, are selective, and all we have that would
> lead us in any different direction is gut instinct. If we're dependent on them
> for analysis, most of the time we go in the direction they recommend.
> Sometimes we do go in a different direction. Then we say that we're giving it
> "the political twist."*

Nor were departmental abilities to gain White House support limited to the
activities of the secretaries, assistant secretaries, and professionals throughout the
agencies, and to White House need for ideas. There were "external" routes to the
White House that did not go through the Domestic Council or the OMB. There
were some risks to the departments in employing such circuitous routes, but such
strategies were used. Two staff members outlined some of these paths:

> *There are some strategies. I'm tempted to say that sandbagging is
> one — having it placed in the press that the department is going to get
> something they're asking for. That apparently happens. Another method is
> to work through interest groups and the relevant committees on the Hill.*

> *Sometimes departments go back through congressional committees. There is
> a kind of open route there, and a kind of closed one. For instance, if you talk
> to [then House Minority Leader] Jerry Ford on something, you know that
> Ford is talking to the White House frequently, and that will feed back. It
> will also feed back at the staff level where the congressional liaison staffs*

> *are talking to the committee staffs or to the individual member's staffs.*
> *There's the public route, talking to newsmen, or talking to special interest*
> *groups and then getting them to come back in. There's clearly the purely*
> *political route, which is going through people who are influential in the*
> *Republican National Committee, or local politicians. A little bit different*
> *than the pure legislative route.*

These external routes were less desirable. A glance back at Figure 3–1 on the relative influence of various persons suggests that if a cabinet member or a Domestic Council staff member became convinced of the wisdom of a policy, its chances of acceptance were greater than if one tried to work through the party or interest groups. But the agency professionals all had policy preferences, and when the elements of the political environment were as closely linked as in Washington, cues about policy were bound to come from many sources.

Now if the department heads were free to make representations directly to the president, or could go through the Domestic Council or the Office of Management and Budget, and if the White House was dependent on the agencies for facts, and was subject to cues about agency preferences coming from many parts of the environment, what latitude was left to Domestic Council staff members to affect policy decisions? One obvious point was that recommendations from the Domestic Council went to the president separately from department recommendations. Cabinet members had an open channel of communication to the president, but so did the Domestic Council staff members. Beyond this, however, there were conditions that permitted aides some influence. These conditions grew out of the interdepartmental nature of many policy decisions.

Policies that affected a single department were relatively rare, and departments often reached divergent conclusions because of their different constituencies and different expertise. This meant that someone outside the departments was going to have to join in the decision-making process. David Archer pointed this out:

> *I could sit right here in this room and watch a fight between the secretary of*
> *labor and the secretary of commerce. According to the secretary of labor,*
> *the inroads of inflation have been such that we're going to have to adopt*
> *policies that allow the workingman greater take-home pay. According to the*
> *secretary of commerce, labor costs must be held down if American business*
> *is going to remain competitive. And because there are no other symbols of*
> *authority, if we have two cabinet officers differing with each other, someone*
> *else is going to have to decide.*

Nancy Schuster called attention to the same situation:

> *When you're in a perspective that you see that one cabinet secretary says*
> *you've got to go this way, it's the only way. And the other secretary says*

> *that the worst thing you can do is to go that way. It has to lower . . . I mean*
> *they become in direct conflict and I would say that I don't make the call on*
> *that. What I do is to say in my report that Secretary A feels very strongly*
> *that the politics, the national interest, the budget, the long-term direction of*
> *the nation requires you to go this way, and he gives a, b, and c as his*
> *reasons. On the other hand, Secretary B says that's not true . . .*

As Miss Schuster began to say, when two cabinet officers found themselves in
opposition to one another, it was likely to lower the influence of both. It certainly
led to a situation where others had to enter the decision-making process.

Bargaining did not always grow out of conflicts between two agencies.
Sometimes decision-making involved several interested parties, and as the process
moved from a two-person zero-sum game to an n-person game in which there were
multiple interests to protect, the procedures became more subtle and more flexible.
As Stuart Leggett pointed out, much White House-department bargaining is both
implicit and complex.

> *I clearly have seen some classic examples of bargaining, almost pure theory*
> *in some situations, where a cabinet secretary may get himself committed*
> *with an outside commitment to the point where he's limited his maneuvera-*
> *bility and negotiation. Then there are kind of trade-offs where we've deter-*
> *mined that this is where we're going to be, but we clearly understand that*
> *someone wants another position, and we're clearly prepared to cave in on*
> *that one in order to get this one. It's played out in very complex ways,*
> *sometimes three-sided . . .*

Sometimes departments signal agreements they have already made. Phrases
such as "This affects our integrity" or "This affects our credibility" are used to
call attention to areas in which they lack maneuverability because they feel they
must uphold a bargain into which they have entered. Sometimes, as Fred Winters
explained, departments are simply concerned about maintaining prerogatives within
their own jurisdictions.

> *I think a certain amount of bargaining goes on because there are so many*
> *overlaps among the three agencies that I'm dealing with. I know that there's*
> *a strong concern in all three departments for their areas of responsibility*
> *and maintaining the lead in their areas of responsibility.*

It is not that there is a simple constituency interest to protect (although this might
also be the case). Rather, each department wants to preserve the right to take future
action itself on any new problems falling within its domain.

If a department was aware that the Domestic Council position was fixed,
and that that position ran counter to its preferences on a given point, it frequently

tried to use their agreement on the one point as a bargaining counter on another. Ted Weber mentioned this:

> *The department comes in and says, here's what we want to do, and we (the staff members) were involved in the writing of the program and the writing of the legislation. So we may have some points where we disagree, and bargaining comes in at that point like any negotiating process. We'll say, why don't you do such and so? And they'll say, we can do it if you'll give us this over here. For instance, in our role a lot of times, we'll say to HUD, we want you to do such and so, and they'll say, well I think we can, but only if you go to OMB and do such and so with them.*

Weber went on to explain that he made an effort to do what he could for the department in such a situation. This was vital in maintaining relations of trust, and helpful in insuring departmental cooperation when it was needed.

> *Sure, I act as broker. I'm probably more easy-going than I ought to be, but I will call and say, particularly in the area of time limits, here's our decision, and we have to have it done by Friday. And the guy'll say, no way we can get it done by Friday. Can it be a week from Friday? I have a relationship with them that I tell them the truth, so I think he's telling me the truth. So I go back up the line and say, he can't do it by then. What's the deal? Most of the time, they'll put it off unless it's something major. If it is, they'll come back and say, no, we have to have it done by Monday. And if I go back to him and say it's Monday, he knows that I've done what I can for him. I know he'll break his back to get it done on time. It's kind of a trade-off.*

Perhaps the most important point about this bargaining is that it was often structured so the president was able to maintain control over the general direction of policy, *and* the Domestic Council staff members were able to insure that the policies were both consistent with his principles and consistent with one another, *and* the departments were able to obtain the results that were important to them. The conditions that made possible this simultaneous achievement of multiple goals were a limited number of presidential preferences in comparison with the number of decisions to be made and a relatively large number of sophisticated bargainers. Lane Redman spoke of one episode that had just those characteristics:

> *One situation that comes to mind is a working group I headed up that had to do with manpower. Three departments were concerned with this in a major way. They were all not necessarily with an institutional position that they had to protect, but with a broad constituency they had to deal with, and so it made a great deal of difference to them and to their constituencies just what*

*course things were going to take, and I would say there was some hauling
and pushing. That resulted in lesser compromises than made a difference to
the president. In other words, the big policy options were not compromised,
so that the president saw less of what the options were. But once the
presidential decisions are made, there are a myriad of details, regulations
and everything else where you can still make trade-offs between departments. The result is that everybody doesn't get killed over something.*

An *n*-person game of this kind is not going to have *n* winners, but there are enough
degrees of freedom that the process does not lead to (*n*-1) losers when the decisions
have been taken.

If a White House decision was of major consequence, it would be communicated to the departments by the president. Many important policy decisions were
also made known to the cabinet members by John Ehrlichman. But, especially on
the details of policy, the Domestic Council staff often communicated the results of
White House deliberations back to the departments. How was this done?

*Oh, very frontal, very direct. We play "president says." And this is very
true. What we say is what he wants done. Most of the people we deal with
know that when we say it, because we don't say it frivolously in this shop. I
can't speak for other shops, but David Archer has been excellent. I think
one reason I have great respect for him is that he doesn't waste, let's say, he
doesn't cry wolf. The result is that when he calls somebody and says, here's
what we want done, they know that is the case.*

The communication of decisions, of course, was a good deal easier when the
departments had been part of the working groups developing the proposals, or when
they had been kept fully informed about the progress of decision-making in the
White House. Two comments suggested the import of both these matters.

*Sometimes we have great success, especially if we decide on something that
is near and dear to a cabinet member's heart.*

*You're always in the position of trying to keep the agencies informed of
what's happening. Nobody's absolutely blissful about the state of affairs at
any given time. They always either tend to think that they should have known
sooner or that they should have known a little more than they did at a
particular time. But you do your best.*

There were times, of course, when a decision was difficult to accept no
matter how many people had advance word of its likelihood. These hard-to-swallow
decisions were apt to involve the cabinet secretary in two ways. First, the secretary

had a clear right of appeal to the president on an adverse decision. Several staff members pointed this out. Mark Jensen, for example, said:

> *I would inform the secretary that the president has made his decision and that it is certainly not something that he wants to impose on everybody without appeal. If they feel that this decision runs contrary to the way that they want to go, that it is one that was not made on the basis of all the facts, that there is new information or new evidence, that they certainly have the right of appeal directly to the president in the form of a memo, or in the form of a direct request for a meeting. . . . I've seen these exact circumstances happen, and I've seen appeals made both with requests for a meeting and with requests to submit a memorandum.*

Appeals of this kind usually dealt with budgetary decisions, but basic policy decisions were sometimes appealed as well. Cabinet members were also likely to be involved if their departments were not sufficiently responsive once a final presidential decision had been made. Asked what action he would take if motion went forward very slowly or imperceptibly, Bruce Frederick replied:

> *Then I'd call up the secretary and I'd say, "We haven't had enough action here. Let's get going."*

Other staff members confirmed that in situations of this kind, they tended to keep their contacts on the secretarial level and let the cabinet members take care of problems within their departments.

In all of this interaction — from initial contact between the agency and the White House through the bargaining on the specifics of policy to the communication of a presidential decision — the best guarantee of good rapport was a sensitivity to the views of the other participants. Frank Miller spoke about his efforts to do this:

> *I think in fairness there is a constant battle to avoid agency paranoia and White House paranoia, and an intelligent approach with reasonably bright people can overcome a good deal of that. You can avoid this developing paranoia that the agencies hate us or they won't do what we want, or that they're out to sandbag us. You can avoid having the agency thinking that the White House is out to get them no matter what they do. Good people, I think, overcome that. Some people don't, and you've got problems when you don't have such good people. But I like to believe that with a conciliatory manner, you're able to sit down and talk with whoever's involved.*

There were, of course, limits to the staff's ability to keep everybody happy. The executive branch is so large, and White House decisions are so important to departmental programs, that Domestic Council staff members could have spent all their time on the phone and still not have been able to relieve everyone's anxiety. What it comes down to is that, with constant effort, concern could be kept within tolerable limits and necessary working relationships in reasonably good repair.

COLLEAGUES

Colleagues on the Domestic Council staff[14] were judged to be nearly as important as cabinet members. As one person put it:

> *Aside from the president's own views, I try to give the utmost consideration to the views of my colleagues, the voters, and the members of the cabinet. Those are the people I'm responsive and responsible to.*

We have already dealt with intragroup influence at some length in Chapter 2, and this topic need not detain us here. One point, however, bears mentioning. It is that the ability of the staff members to be persuasive with their colleagues rested on the fact that each was understood to be grappling with the same complex environment. As Norm McCullough explained:

> *When I say that the judgment of my colleagues makes a very great differ-ence, I'm assuming they've already analyzed the inputs of the interest groups, they've analyzed the mood of the Congress, they've analyzed the views of the cabinet that are pertinent in that field. So if I'm talking to them, I've already got these other inputs, or they've got these other inputs, and when I'm basing my judgment on the value of their input, I'm assuming that they're kind of at the end of the road, the end of the pipeline, and they've already had all this other stuff pass by them.*

CONGRESS

Contact between the Congress and the Domestic Council was somewhat restricted, and the influence of the legislative leadership tended to be somewhat specialized. Legislation, it was explained, left the White House

> *. . . on two tracks. The lead track is the department. There is always a department responsible for the progress of the legislation. The presidential Legislative Liaison staff looks after the legislation, and the Domestic Coun-cil Assistant Director looks after the department.*

Therefore the amount of contact with the Congress was very much a function of whether new legislation was needed for the policies being handled in a particular shop. If so, contact with the Hill was apt to be continuous. If not, months could go by in which the staff member's attention was focused elsewhere.

The influence of congressional leaders depended on the point a bill had reached in the legislative process. Not surprisingly, congressional voices were most apt to be authoritative when compromise was the only way to obtain needed votes. Mary Hickman commented on this:

> *If we're at a point in the legislative process, and we are in the Congress and there's substantial dispute about a particular policy matter or direction, then it could be that some of the congressional views would make a very great difference. If you really want to achieve something, and the question is what's the best way to do this, then we may have to bend something that we would otherwise not prefer to do.*

Congressional influence was also particularized because of the nature of legislative responsibilities. Legislators were perceived as having detailed understanding of the matters coming before their committees, but less capacity to make determinations when two policy areas were competing for the same resources. In this respect legislators and agency personnel had similar roles. They were seen as advocates for constituency interests, and, while they were respected in that capacity, this very advocacy limited their ability to determine overall priorities. David Archer spoke about the distinctive nature of legislative competence.

> *If you're in a specialized area, they're very good in a specialized area. But they're totally unknowledgeable when it comes to priorities, to priority-setting outside their own subcommittee work.*

Ward Norris made a closely related point.

> *There are instances where the president, in terms of his authority with respect to the office of the president, his inherent powers, might impound some money in order to keep within a spending ceiling. Here the views of the legislative leadership would make relatively little difference.*

Although Norris, a lawyer, was calling attention to a legal basis for presidential action, other comments suggested that his perception was the same as that of his colleagues. Congressmen were seen as having specific roles to play. At particular times, and on particular issues, they were the most important source of cues to the Domestic Council staff. In general, though, legislators were less important than the political and policy advocates in the executive branch.[15]

INTEREST GROUPS

There is no question about the confined nature of the influence that was exercised by interest group spokesmen, bureau chiefs, or Republican party leaders. All of them were listened to, but the average influence scores for these categories are quite a bit lower than those for actors we have discussed thus far. In each case, a person had to have some additional credentials (beyond being just an interest group spokesman or just a party leader) if he was to be considered a potent source of policy cues.

There was a clear differentiation among interest groups on the basis of the tactics they followed. Many staff members commented on this. For example, Carl Baker said:

> *There are some interest groups who are organized and can do something. There are some other interest groups that can't do anything but scream. There are interest groups like the National League of Cities-National Conference of Mayors, who when they come in here give you a sheet of paper that tells you exactly what they're going to do or what they're going to say, a week before. When they come in to talk to you, you know where they are, and you know what the issues are. There are other interest groups that inundate you with nasty phone calls, and demonstrations out in front of the White House, and they probably make no difference at all.*

An interest group's past relationships with the Domestic Council staff also made a difference. If an interest group had given helpful advice on one point, it might become a valued source of cues. Dan Bailey spoke about this possibility at some length.

> *I come in contact with a lot of interest groups, whether I want to or not. They volunteer their services. They're always knocking at my door. Some of them are billing the company for the time they're able to spend in the White House. And they'll come just to be able to say they're here. There are others who I, through working with them, come to know have a pretty good sense of things. We make a decision. We come out in a particular point of view. This is the way that the special interest guy suggested. He said you're going to take a little bit of flak if you go this way, but not a whole lot. If you go the other way, you'll get creamed. Then I have a feeling about how that guy tends to come out. I then respect him more as an advisor, someone who has a philosophical attunement and a good sense of how the reaction will be.*

Not surprisingly, interest groups exerted more influence when they knew enough about Domestic Council habits to be able to work with them in a supportive fashion.

BUREAU CHIEFS

Domestic Council staff members often linked interest group spokesmen and bureau chiefs in their discussion. There were several references to ''the Iron Triangle'' or ''the Triple Alliance,'' the mutually supportive relationship of interest groups, bureaus, and the relevant committees on the Hill. Another similarity between interest group spokesmen and bureau chiefs was the variation in influence from person to person. Alan Hampton remarked that it was difficult to give a simple answer about the importance of agency heads:

> *That's tough because they're all over the map. There are some bureau chiefs that make a very great difference. There are guys that run agencies like the Social Security Administration, which is a bureau of HEW, who have immense responsibilities. There are some bureau chiefs who probably make no difference at all. So, in that category, I'd say that they range from very great to none at all. And I would probably say that same kind of thing . . . Interest groups probably have the same sort of impact on me that bureau chiefs do, and for similar reasons.*

Two of Hampton's colleagues pointed to bureau chiefs as sources of particular influence because of their detailed, professional knowledge within specific areas.

> *Bureau chiefs are even more knowledgeable than the cabinet officers, but within a narrower range.*

> *The bureau chief must be understood in terms of what his interests are. I wouldn't discredit his factual representations at all, but I would discredit his political sensibilities somewhat.*

Thus, the rules of the game were rather similar for bureau chiefs and for interest group spokesmen. Both exerted limited influence,[16] and both were in a position to do so because they had the specific expertise needed for policy determination. Some bureau chiefs and some interest group spokesmen, specifically those who understood the use of information as a means of influence, were able to cultivate relationships that allowed them to become actors of real importance.

REPUBLICAN PARTY LEADERS

Party leaders were also among those who needed additional credentials if their word was to carry weight with Domestic Council staff members. Few respondents went so far as one who denied knowing any Republican party leaders (aside from the legislative leaders). but the mean influence scores were the lowest recorded. A typical comment was that of Frank Miller. He asked the same kinds of questions about the hypothetical party leaders' credentials that he would concerning anyone else who wanted to affect policy.

> *You're talking about somebody solely in his position as a Republican party leader? If his only qualification is that he's a Republican party leader, I would say hardly any difference. I rely a lot on outside people, and I bring in people, professors or lawyers or other people. With all of these people, the weight you give somebody's opinion depends . . . I have trouble with somebody that's solely a Republican party leader.*

Nancy Schuster also raised questions about the individual's qualifications; specifically, whether he was one who had given you accurate information in the past.

> *I'd have to put them in the same category as special interest groups. Some will come in and say, you're going to sink in my state if you do this. You're going to sink me. You're going to sink everybody that runs for Congress hereafter and the state legislature. And they're dead wrong. He's just giving me his own personal point of view. And you have to know whether this guy is really sensitive to feelings in his state, whether he's with you, and whether he has built up credibility for giving you good information.*

Some party leaders were listened to by the Domestic Council staff, but before that happened, personal judgments had to be made about the quality of information they were able to convey.

Two other things should be borne in mind in considering this apparent lack of impact by party leaders. One is that, as was the case with Congress, there was another staff (headed by Harry Dent) that maintained liaison with the Republican party. Hence messages about political impact would be relayed through other White House channels (e.g., "This is important in New Jersey") rather than coming directly from party leaders. The other consideration is that a political party is more important as a source of recruitment than a channel of communication. One party leader is propelled into the presidency, and a few more are appointed by him to positions in the cabinet, subcabinet, and White House staff. This handful is not a random sample of the whole party; almost all are drawn from the nomination and electoral coalitions that supported the successful candidate. Once they are in office, they are almost immediately preoccupied with policy questions that cross their desks. In order to come to grips with their new responsibilities, they need to talk with persons who have expert knowledge in those substantive areas—not their erstwhile party colleagues. To the extent that the president and his staff have attitudes that are representative of the party, the policies decided upon after these explorations are likely to be generally acceptable to the party. The details of these policies, however, will depend on the facts they have discovered. They will not opt for a specific provision because it is thought to be "Republican" while another is "Democratic." Nor will a decision be made just because a party leader from a certain state drops by the White House for a quiet conversation. Consequently, if party influence is to be detected, one must look at the general tone of policy, and in a policy area where there are significant partisan differences.

MORE OF THE VIEW FROM THE WHITE HOUSE

Let us return now to the question of how the Domestic Council staff adapted to this complex environment. We have been reviewing the actors with whom they came in contact one at a time; but the staff did not receive its cues this way. As they worked on their policy assignments they heard from all the participants. The elements of their environment were not only interrelated, but they had to be dealt with simultaneously. How did that affect staff attitudes?

There were some general attitudes[17] (as opposed to views in specific policy areas) that seemed to be affected by the environment as it was seen from the White House. It would not be proper to call *all* of these group norms; there was not enough staff agreement on a couple of points. But it would be accurate to say that new approaches were welcomed by the staff, and new federal programs were not. They believed that breadth of view was more likely to be found in the White House than elsewhere, and they were skeptical about whether the government could be managed from the White House.

These generalizations are based on the staff responses presented in Table 3–4. The extent of disagreement with the idea of new federal programs was suggested by one aide who laughed (as he indicated his own strong disagreement) and said, "If anybody gives a different answer to this, he's fired!" This opposition to new federal programs, though, was based on beliefs that the federal government was already too powerful, that it made too many demands on existing resources, and that it might be too unwieldy to be managed—not on an opposition to new ideas. In fact, there was nearly as strong disagreement with the notion that new approaches weren't worth the effort. The total staff consensus on this point was striking, since they knew from immediate personal experience just how much work was necessary to get new endeavors accepted.

As between the White House and other agencies, the Domestic Council staff believed that breadth of vision was more likely to be found in the Executive Mansion. An almost grudging acceptance of these beliefs was suggested by such comments as "Sad, but true," and "It shouldn't be that way, but it is." Perhaps the most interesting finding, though, was a lack of agreement about whether the federal government could be managed. The statement about the size and complexity of the federal establishment caused one of the most experienced leaders to pause for a long time and say, "This is a very complex question." The item about the adequacy of presidential resources led Ted Weber to remark, "This is why the meetings at

TABLE 3-4
General Attitudes of Staff Members

	. *Mean Score**
"The best way to deal with an emerging problem is to create a new federal program."	1.44
"New ways of doing things usually aren't worth the work to get them accepted."	1.69
"Civil servants have the narrow perspectives of their own agencies."	5.25
"Members of the White House staff have broader perspectives than other agencies."	5.31
"The White House has adequate resources to impose presidential priorities on the government."	3.81
"The federal government is too large and too complex for effective coordination."	4.56

*Low scores indicate disagreement; high scores indicate agreement. For further information, see Appendix A3.9.

Camp David (on governmental reorganization, held immediately after the 1972 election) are taking so long." David Archer, after a long sigh, replied, "I'll know in four more years. OK?" Responses on both these items ran all the way from "strongly disagree" to "strongly agree." The lack of consensus on a capacity to govern — after four years of trying to do just that — tells something about the relative complexity of the political environment in which the White House is situated, and gives a different perspective to questions about the growth in presidential power. Much has been written about the increasing power of the presidency. Such assertions are quite true in an absolute sense. Lyndon Johnson and Richard Nixon were more powerful presidents than, say, Calvin Coolidge and Herbert Hoover. Statements about the growth of presidential power are also accurate if one compares the authority acquired by the White House in recent decades with new power that has come to the Congress. But if one asks whether the president and his aides have sufficient influence to respond to all the challenges they face, the answer is different. For example, Richard Neustadt spoke about the difficulties facing John F. Kennedy in 1962:

> *He does not have effective power in the sense of assured support. He doesn't*
> *have this with Congress. Everybody can see that. He doesn't have assured*
> *support from within the executive branch, because all government officials*
> *have to think about congressional committees from which they get their*
> *money. He clearly doesn't have assured support from particular private*
> *groups and organizations within the society. . . . It's not sufficiently*

TABLE 3-4
General Attitudes of Staff Members

	Mean Score*
"The best way to deal with an emerging problem is to create a new federal program."	1.44
"New ways of doing things usually aren't worth the work to get them accepted."	1.69
"Civil servants have the narrow perspectives of their own agencies."	5.25
"Members of the White House staff have broader perspectives than other agencies."	5.31
"The White House has adequate resources to impose presidential priorities on the government."	3.81
"The federal government is too large and too complex for effective coordination."	4.56

*Low scores indicate disagreement; high scores indicate agreement. For further information, see Appendix A3.9.

Camp David (on governmental reorganization, held immediately after the 1972 election) are taking so long.'' David Archer, after a long sigh, replied, "I'll know in four more years. OK?'' Responses on both these items ran all the way from "strongly disagree'' to "strongly agree.'' The lack of consensus on a capacity to govern—after four years of trying to do just that—tells something about the relative complexity of the political environment in which the White House is situated, and gives a different perspective to questions about the growth in presidential power. Much has been written about the increasing power of the presidency. Such assertions are quite true in an absolute sense. Lyndon Johnson and Richard Nixon were more powerful presidents than, say, Calvin Coolidge and Herbert Hoover. Statements about the growth of presidential power are also accurate if one compares the authority acquired by the White House in recent decades with new power that has come to the Congress. But if one asks whether the president and his aides have sufficient influence to respond to all the challenges they face, the answer is different. For example, Richard Neustadt spoke about the difficulties facing John F. Kennedy in 1962:

> He does not have effective power in the sense of assured support. He doesn't have this with Congress. Everybody can see that. He doesn't have assured support from within the executive branch, because all government officials have to think about congressional committees from which they get their money. He clearly doesn't have assured support from particular private groups and organizations within the society. . . . It's not sufficiently

BUREAU CHIEFS

Domestic Council staff members often linked interest group spokesmen and bureau chiefs in their discussion. There were several references to "the Iron Triangle'' or "the Triple Alliance,'' the mutually supportive relationship of interest groups, bureaus, and the relevant committees on the Hill. Another similarity between interest group spokesmen and bureau chiefs was the variation in influence from person to person. Alan Hampton remarked that it was difficult to give a simple answer about the importance of agency heads:

> That's tough because they're all over the map. There are some bureau chiefs that make a very great difference. There are guys that run agencies like the Social Security Administration, which is a bureau of HEW, who have immense responsibilities. There are some bureau chiefs who probably make no difference at all. So, in that category, I'd say that they range from very great to none at all. And I would probably say that same kind of thing . . . Interest groups probably have the same sort of impact on me that bureau chiefs do, and for similar reasons.

Two of Hampton's colleagues pointed to bureau chiefs as sources of particular influence because of their detailed, professional knowledge within specific areas.

> Bureau chiefs are even more knowledgeable than the cabinet officers, but within a narrower range.

> The bureau chief must be understood in terms of what his interests are. I wouldn't discredit his factual representations at all, but I would discredit his political sensibilities somewhat.

Thus, the rules of the game were rather similar for bureau chiefs and for interest group spokesmen. Both exerted limited influence,[16] and both were in a position to do so because they had the specific expertise needed for policy determination. Some bureau chiefs and some interest group spokesmen, specifically those who understood the use of information as a means of influence, were able to cultivate relationships that allowed them to become actors of real importance.

REPUBLICAN PARTY LEADERS

Party leaders were also among those who needed additional credentials if their word was to carry weight with Domestic Council staff members. Few respondents went so far as one who denied knowing any Republican party leaders (aside from the legislative leaders). but the mean influence scores were the lowest recorded. A typical comment was that of Frank Miller. He asked the same kinds of questions about the hypothetical party leaders' credentials that he would concerning anyone else who wanted to affect policy.

> *You're talking about somebody solely in his position as a Republican party leader? If his only qualification is that he's a Republican party leader, I would say hardly any difference. I rely a lot on outside people, and I bring in people, professors or lawyers or other people. With all of these people, the weight you give somebody's opinion depends . . . I have trouble with somebody that's solely a Republican party leader.*

Nancy Schuster also raised questions about the individual's qualifications; specifically, whether he was one who had given you accurate information in the past.

> *I'd have to put them in the same category as special interest groups. Some will come in and say, you're going to sink in my state if you do this. You're going to sink me. You're going to sink everybody that runs for Congress hereafter and the state legislature. And they're dead wrong. He's just giving me his own personal point of view. And you have to know whether this guy is really sensitive to feelings in his state, whether he's with you, and whether he has built up credibility for giving you good information.*

Some party leaders were listened to by the Domestic Council staff, but before that happened, personal judgments had to be made about the quality of information they were able to convey.

Two other things should be borne in mind in considering this apparent lack of impact by party leaders. One is that, as was the case with Congress, there was another staff (headed by Harry Dent) that maintained liaison with the Republican party. Hence messages about political impact would be relayed through other White House channels (e.g., "This is important in New Jersey") rather than coming directly from party leaders. The other consideration is that a political party is more important as a source of recruitment than a channel of communication. One party leader is propelled into the presidency, and a few more are appointed by him to positions in the cabinet, subcabinet, and White House staff. This handful is not a random sample of the whole party; almost all are drawn from the nomination and electoral coalitions that supported the successful candidate. Once they are in office, they are almost immediately preoccupied with policy questions that cross their desks. In order to come to grips with their new responsibilities, they need to talk with persons who have expert knowledge in those substantive areas—not their erstwhile party colleagues. To the extent that the president and his staff have attitudes that are representative of the party, the policies decided upon after these explorations are likely to be generally acceptable to the party. The details of these policies, however, will depend on the facts they have discovered. They will not opt

for a specific provision because it is thought to be "Republican [...] "Democratic." Nor will a decision be made just because a par[...] certain state drops by the White House for a quiet conversation. [...] party influence is to be detected, one must look at the general tone o[...] a policy area where there are significant partisan differences.

MORE OF THE VIEW FROM THE WHITE HOUSE

Let us return now to the question of how the Domestic Council staff adapte[...] complex environment. We have been reviewing the actors with whom they c[...] contact one at a time; but the staff did not receive its cues this way. As they w[...] on their policy assignments they heard from all the participants. The elemen[...] their environment were not only interrelated, but they had to be dealt with sim[...] taneously. How did that affect staff attitudes?

There were some general attitudes[17] (as opposed to views in specific polic[...] areas) that seemed to be affected by the environment as it was seen from the White House. It would not be proper to call *all* of these group norms; there was not enough staff agreement on a couple of points. But it would be accurate to say that new approaches were welcomed by the staff, and new federal programs were not. They believed that breadth of view was more likely to be found in the White House than elsewhere, and they were skeptical about whether the government could be managed from the White House.

These generalizations are based on the staff responses presented in Table 3–4. The extent of disagreement with the idea of new federal programs was suggested by one aide who laughed (as he indicated his own strong disagreement) and said, "If anybody gives a different answer to this, he's fired!" This opposition to new federal programs, though, was based on beliefs that the federal government was already too powerful, that it made too many demands on existing resources, and that it might be too unwieldy to be managed—not on an opposition to new ideas. In fact, there was nearly as strong disagreement with the notion that new approaches weren't worth the effort. The total staff consensus on this point was striking, since they knew from immediate personal experience just how much work was necessary to get new endeavors accepted.

As between the White House and other agencies, the Domestic Council staff believed that breadth of vision was more likely to be found in the Executive Mansion. An almost grudging acceptance of these beliefs was suggested by such comments as "Sad, but true," and "It shouldn't be that way, but it is." Perhaps the most interesting finding, though, was a lack of agreement about whether the federal government could be managed. The statement about the size and complexity of the federal establishment caused one of the most experienced leaders to pause for a long time and say, "This is a very complex question." The item about the adequacy of presidential resources led Ted Weber to remark, "This is why the meetings at *realized that the President's position is comparable to the situation of a cat on a hot tin roof. This man is always having to grab for just enough power to get by the next day's problems.*[18]

A decade later, Domestic Council staff member Stuart Leggett spoke in a similar way about the limitations of power when viewed from a White House perspective:

People see things from different vantage points. Those outside think the White House can do anything it wants to. The White House tends to move by an aggregate sense of what's possible and what it thinks it can live with.

To those working in the White House the crucial question is the balance between the resources at their disposal and the complexity of the environment in which they are situated. The White House is not without means of influencing others, but it certainly is not the master of its environment. The result is that staff members must cope with constant challenges.

If the political environment is such that not everything can be done, it is well to ask what absolutely must be done. To ascertain those institutional imperatives, staff members were asked: "What would you say are the things the Council *must* do in order to serve the needs of the president?" One answer was heard over and over again:

The job the Council must do is to clarify the president's options.

To make sure that we have done the best job possible of determining the facts and alternative solutions when the president has to make a decision.

This view arose from two considerations. First, most staff members believed that the decisions made by a president were the most crucial thing in determining the success or failure of an administration. Second, they understood that the president's time was even more limited than their own. Therefore the role of the Domestic Council was to scan the environment, determine the possibilities, and communicate those to the president so he could make informed decisions without having to make impossible investments of his own time. As Ward Norris said:

The first thing I'd say is to be able to write as simply and concisely as possible. In other words, give him a range of options, but do it without his having to read through reams and reams of material, and without his having to become an expert in any particular field. We do this by applying our judgment, and our judgment as experts in the field.

The end product was a simple option paper, but: All possible options had to be included. There had to be documentation about the alternatives. The reactions of agencies that might be affected had to be ascertained. The relationships between programs being proposed and existing legislation had to be explored. And estimates of the political reactions of various groups had to be set forth. This meant that hundreds of hours of staff time had to be expended in order to save precious time on the presidential schedule. Mark Jensen spoke about the work required by these institutional imperatives:

> *The must part of it is that we must explore all possible, even the dead-end, routes, and tell him why they're dead-end, at least cover the waterfront in the case of disgorging information and know how much it will cost and what implications it has with respect to existing government programs or programs operated by state or local governments or how it will conflict with other government agencies. In any conflicts, including the conflicts of special interest groups, we are making an appraisal — although there's a separate staff for actually giving us a more informed appraisal of how well it'll sail in Congress. In this form, it'll never fly; in slightly tinkered form it will. There's one guy on the committee who just won't buy that provision, and there's no point in trying to get it through. But our job is to make sure that there is not simply a single point of view being presented, so that the president does know, even if he's made a wrong choice, that at least it's with conscious knowledge of what the consequences will be. And nobody's so omniscient as to be able to determine all the possibilities, but our function is to be as exhaustive as we can be.*

Since the job was to be as exhaustive as possible, it follows that sources of information were needed. Some of the information was written down — existing statutes, for example — but most of the estimates about implications of programs and the likely political consequences of adopting them came from other actors with whom the staff came in contact. Fred Winters saw a need for communication that was functionally related to clarifying options.

> *Well, I think the biggest must is that we must be able to communicate with the right people. We must have the freedom to go inside government, outside government, wherever it happens to be, to get inputs that are going to present all of the views on a particular circumstance or a particular problem, so we're not handing the president decision papers that are not balanced papers.*

Yet there was more to the acquisition of information than simple communication. It would be better stated as necessary communication in conjunction with an equally essential understanding of how the many players in this game of politics were interacting with one another. What was needed was not simple information, but information interpreted in the light of a mastery of Washington politics. Such a knowledge of the political environment was most likely to come from experience. Ralph Schmidt spoke about just this point:

> *The Domestic Council has got to be able to understand the various positions on policy. The simple ones, of course, are the positions taken by the agencies, the positions taken by the other elements of the White House, OMB, OST, or whatever. In a more complex fashion, one must understand where the interest groups are, and this gets very hairy sometimes because the interest groups in this city are extremely skillful. They've been at it a hell of a long time. They've made great inroads in the Congress and in the agencies. I know people of long experience talk about the triple alliance that has always existed between the congressional committees and their staffs, the congressmen, the portion of the federal agency that is essentially owned by the interest groups whose programs are theirs, and the special interest groups. And to really do a job in this place, you've got to do the best you can to understand what the relationship is. We've gone through a real education on this.*

In such a context, "isolated" decision-making in the White House is impossible.

SUMMARY

The actors who composed the political environment in which the Domestic Council staff was situated could be distinguished into three broad classes, according to the influence they exercised. The president was the most important; a second grouping—voters, cabinet members, staff colleagues, and (to a lesser extent) legislative leaders—exercised a general influence; members of a third grouping—interest group spokesmen, bureau chiefs, and Republican party leaders—were able to make their voices heard under specific conditions. The Domestic Council staff was thrust into continual contact with elements of this environment by their own institutional imperatives. They had to contact others in order to obtain information needed by the president. They had to understand the intricate relationships between the others to see the implications of the courses of action they recommended. And once a presidential decision was made, the staff had to contact the other actors again to explain the policy and aid in implementing it.

NOTES

[1]Heinz Eulau and Kenneth Prewitt, *Labyrinths of Democracy* (Indianapolis: Bobbs-Merrill, 1973), p. 80.

[2]*Labyrinths of Democracy*, p. 126.

[3]For a discussion of how the relative influence of the various actors was determined, see Appendix A3.1.

[4]For a description of the measures of staff perceptions of President Nixon's attitudes, see Appendix A3.2.

[5]Civil liberties was an exception to this. Here the two items tended in opposite directions. When compared with the staff members dealing with matters in this policy area, President Nixon was seen as more opposed to the use of government power to compel busing (1.50 v. 2.00), and more in favor of increasing police authority (4.13 v. 3.38).

[6]For a discussion of the measure of consensus used, see Appendix A3.3.

[7]These data came from a study directed by my colleague, C. Richard Hofstetter. I should like to thank Professor Hofstetter for making these preliminary data available for this analysis. For a brief description of the data, see Appendix A3.4.

[8]For information on the wording of the interview items on staff perceptions of the general public, see Appendix A3.5.

[9]For a discussion of this measure, see Appendix A3.6.

[10]For a discussion of this measure, see Appendix A3.7.

[11]Another possibility is that relatively inexperienced aides who were aware of their own lack of information about what motivated voters simply took the word of more senior White House personnel that voters preferred less government activity. We have no data that would enable us to test this hypothesis one way or the other.

[12]For a study showing that misperception tends to move judgments in the direction of one's own attitudes, see R. M. W. Travers, "A Study in Judging the Opinions of Groups," *Archives of Psychology*, December, 1941, pp. 5–73; for an argument that one tends to perceive by using his most accessible cognitive category, see Jerome Bruner, "On Perceptual Readiness," *Psychological Review*, 1957, pp. 123–152. For a correlation analysis of the relationship between staff attitudes, staff perception of the voters' attitudes, and the voters' attitudes, see Appendix A3.8.

[13]When a problem was important enough to call for a cabinet committee (a subcommittee of the Domestic Council), the committee was chaired by a cabinet member, and the working group responsible for drafting proposals was chaired by a Domestic Council staff member. The cabinet member had the authority of legitimacy; the Domestic Council staff member had the authority of expertise.

[14]There is a small logical problem in including the staff as part of the staff's own environment. On the group level, this is logically impossible. On the individual level, however, other staff members are very much part of the environment to which the person responds.

[15]Remember that there is another staff, the Legislative Liaison, for whom those on the Hill are the most important external groups. Legislative Liaison personnel may relay information to the Domestic Council staff.

[16]What is limited influence from a White House perspective may be quite sufficient to protect the more limited concerns of an interest group or agency. One thoughtful staff member said: "There is some policy-making, but there's a good deal more program-tinkering. On the level of program-tinkering, we're not prime participants. I think the prime

participants would be found elsewhere. They would be found among people in the subcommittees on the Hill, people in the bureau level in the agencies and departments, in private interest groups, and among certain policy leaders that are at least outside of official government."

[17]For discussion of these general attitudes, see Appendix A3.9.

[18]"Size-up of Kennedy in the White House," in *U.S. News and World Report*, July 16, 1962, p. 60.

Chapter 4

Activities of the Council

The Domestic Council was given a very broad mandate when it was created. Indeed, the responsibilities mentioned in President Nixon's message to the Congress[1] suggested a comprehensive bureaucratic activity that would serve every policy need from the first glimmer of a social problem through an exhaustive evaluation of the ultimate government response. The Domestic Council was to engage in the collection of information, determination of national goals, identification of policies by which those goals might be obtained, assignment of priorities among competing activities, and monitoring of programs that had already been set in motion. Added to this systematic sequence of evaluation-decision-implementation was a reference to emergency assignments. The Council was to provide "rapid response to presidential needs for policy advice on pressing domestic issues."

An equally sweeping interpretation of Domestic Council activities was given by one of the leaders, David Archer:

> There isn't anything in the domestic area that we don't handle, and when we set this up we defined domestic as anything that wasn't obviously foreign. So there's quite a range. Busing. Housing. Use your imagination. Anything that is domestic, and this means anything that's obviously not foreign. There's one important qualification I should add here: anything that's domestic that merits the president's attention.

The problem with both the charter and this claim was that they were too comprehensive. The list of activities was simply too long. The claim that the Council handled everything in the domestic area was simply too broad. No staff of 28 was going to be able to carry out such a mandate. What these statements do tell us is that President Nixon could use the Council in any way he saw fit. Its authorization was sufficiently broad that the Council could not be challenged by a claim that a given activity went beyond its charter. That leaves us, of course, with the question of how the president chose to use his Domestic Council. Specifically, what were the staff members doing with their time?

The answer is that the Domestic Council staff was most involved in decision-making, spending a fair amount of time on emergency activities, and least involved in gathering intelligence and monitoring the bureaucracy. When asked directly how they were spending their time,[2] they ranked the activities from most time-consuming to least time-consuming as follows: clarifying options among issues being presented for decision, backstopping the president by "fire-engine" chores when answers were needed in a hurry, determining priorities to govern the use of presently available resources, collecting information and developing long-range forecasts on national needs, and monitoring agency activity to be fully aware of the ways on going programs were being administered.

This pattern of activity on the part of the Council staff reflects the leaders' use of their time. As a glance at Table 4–1 will show, there was an important distinction between the time allocations of leaders and aides. Every leader's attention was fixed on the central task of clarifying options. They were also making a fair

TABLE 4–1
Mean Time Allocations of Domestic Council Staff Members

Activity	Time Use*	
	Leaders	Aides
Clarifying options	4.00	3.31
Determining priorities	3.33	2.67
Backstopping the president	3.33	2.71
Collecting information	2.33	2.67
Monitoring agencies	2.00	2.75

*High figures represent greater expenditure of time; low figures mean less use of time. For explanation of the meaning of the figures, see Appendix A4.1.

number of decisions themselves as well as responding to "fire-engine" calls to help the president. The leaders were not spending much time gathering information for long-range forecasts, and still less to following agency activity. Staff aides had a different pattern of responsibilities. They, too, were more concerned with clarifying options than with anything else, but there were no meaningful time distinctions among the other four tasks. Thus, the leaders were spending more time than aides on the high-priority tasks of clarifying options, determining priorities, and backstopping the president. The aides were spending more time than the leaders gathering information and monitoring agency activity. To the extent that the lower-priority tasks were receiving Domestic Council attention, it was coming from the lower-ranking staff members.

There was also considerable variation in the amount of attention devoted to the six issue areas. The overall allocation of staff time (with mean time use figures in parentheses) was: social benefits (3.32), economic management (2.89), civil liberties (2.16), natural resources (1.89), international involvement (1.63), and agriculture (1.58).[3] Not surprisingly, the major domestic policy areas, social benefits and economic management, took more of the staff's attention, and the minor domestic policy areas required somewhat less. International involvement was an interesting case because it suggests the extent to which "foreign policy" and "domestic policy" mesh on the operating level. None of the Domestic Council staff members was spending as much as "a fair amount of time" on international matters; yet the work of many people was affected in one way or another by foreign activities. There had been an international conference on the environment in Stockholm, the Peace Corps was funded through the budget of the ACTION agency, some questions about transatlantic air travel fell under transportation, the discharge of Vietnam veterans affected the employment picture, and so forth. "Domestic policy" is no more insulated from the effects of foreign events than "foreign policy" can be conducted without reference to domestic political support.

The kinds of things the staff members were doing depended to some degree on the policy areas in which they were active. The mean time use figures by policy area are given in Table 4–2. The allocations of staff attention for the major policy areas, social benefits and economic management, followed the overall pattern for the staff.[4] But this was not true of civil liberties, natural resources, and agriculture. Those dealing with civil liberties were spending as much time responding to emergency situations as they were in clarifying options, and they were giving more attention to what the agencies were doing than were staff members in any other policy area. Conversely, they were less apt to determine priorities themselves. When dealing with politically explosive issues such as busing and integration, this

TABLE 4–2
Mean Staff Time Allocations by Issue Area

Activity	Time Use*				
	Economic manage- ment	Social benefits	Civil liberties	Natural resources	Agri- culture
Clarifying options	3.64	3.50	3.37	3.60	3.75
Determining priorities	3.08	2.87	2.50	3.80	3.75
Backstopping the president	3.23	3.00	3.37	3.20	3.50
Collecting information	2.62	2.67	2.37	2.20	2.50
Monitoring agencies	2.64	2.47	2.75	2.60	2.25

*High figures represent greater expenditure of time; low figures mean less use of time. For explanation of the meaning of the figures, see Appendixes A4.1 and A4.2.

evidence suggests that crucial decisions were being made on a higher level, and staff members were following governmental activity closely to be aware of developing problems as quickly as possible. In the less important areas of natural resources and agriculture,[5] there was a different pattern. Here the staff members were spending as much time making decisions themselves as they were in clarifying choices to be made by John Ehrlichman or the president, but they spent little time following agency activity or gathering information.

CLARIFYING OPTIONS

Every bit of evidence points to the clarification of options among issues being presented for decision as the central responsibility of the Domestic Council staff. The views of staff members about institutional imperatives that we reviewed at the end of Chapter 3, the time use data we have just seen, the examples given by the staff members of activities in which they were engaged, and the obvious pride with which staff members spoke of their involvement in presidential decision-making all call our attention to it above all other duties assigned to the Council. Furthermore, the sequence of activities involved—initiation of a project, heading a working group, preliminary decisions, further refinement, final approval, and public announcement—is at the very heart of presidential politics. Hence clarifying options merits our close attention.

There was no single pattern typical of all the Council did to clarify questions for the president. There were times problems emerged so quickly that they were simply talked out among staff members; there were others when months of staff consultation and study preceded the submission of a formal option paper. One often-followed sequence was set in the development of the Family Assistance Plan in the summer preceding the creation of the Domestic Council.[6]

> *This was really the project that created the pattern for the Domestic Council. The president knew generally what he wanted on this. He set down general guidelines. He knew that if the current system was projected, it was going to go bust. It would bankrupt the system. I was the person who headed up the task force on this. I had assistant secretaries from Labor, HEW, someone from Budget, and one person from Moynihan's staff, and one person from Burns's staff. I don't mean to say that we did it all. We had departmental backup. We got figures from Labor, from HEW, from OEO. They had the best computer runs at the time, results of the experiments, and so forth. . . . The president gave his speech in mid-August. I worked day and night on that from . . . The last time I remember celebrating was the Fourth of July weekend. I worked steadily from that time until the speech was given.*

This general process was to be repeated a number of times when major decisions were before the Domestic Council. First, there would be some general guidance from the president giving his views on the matter. Then a task group would be created with personnel from the departments concerned and other units (especially OMB) within the Executive Office of the President. This task group, whose working head was a Domestic Council staff member, often met first with a range of persons interested in the problem, then confined discussion to its own membership as the group began to get a better feel for the problem. These discussions would lead to a preliminary major decision, often in the form of an option paper, about the general policies to be followed. Then there would be a follow-up period, sometimes with intensive interaction with the president, while details of the program were being worked out. Finally, there would be a public statement of some kind announcing the policies that had been decided upon.

The initial instructions often originated with the president, but they were likely to reach the person who would carry out the assignment through John Ehrlichman or Kenneth Cole. Scott Manning recalled one such instance:

> *There are certain things on which the president wants results and has designated Domestic Council staff to work on them. For example, crime in the central cities. The president read the first quarter crime statistics at Camp David one weekend. On Monday, he told John Ehrlichman that this had to stop. John told Norm McCullough that something had to happen on this or else the president was going to want a pretty good explanation; the full resources of the federal government were to be made available.*

Others remembered receiving their marching orders in similar ways.

> *I was given this job in August. I was told to be in charge of preparing a presidential message and to get going on the issue.*

> *Just briefly, over a year ago we could see the problem of confusion because of all the court orders. The president asked members of the cabinet to begin looking at things, and we began working with the various agency personnel in almost a project way. Ultimately, this resulted in the president's legislative proposal.*

A project could be self-initiated. If a staff member saw an emerging problem in his area, and called it to the attention of John Ehrlichman or Kenneth Cole, he might be told to get busy and work something up on it. Presidential interest, however, was a guarantee of action, and was much more likely to result in a formal task group being set up to work on the matter.

The membership of the task groups obviously depended on the problem being addressed. Generally, it would be accurate to think of them as including

Domestic Council staff members, representatives from various agencies in the Executive Office of the President, and still others from the departments concerned. The reports of the participants, though, are better for conveying the flavor of the task group activity. Bart Compton recalled one he had been associated with:

> I don't know all the names. I had been here only a short time myself, but I think there were two assistant directors of the Office of Management and Budget. I'm not sure if the head of the health unit in OMB was in it or not. An assistant secretary at HEW was the agency guy, and most of the people that were very active in it were in his office. The under secretary was in and out of it, and there was another assistant secretary at HEW who was in it sometimes, so there you have pretty much the main actors in it. All of the working groups have had congressional liaison types, both from the agency and from the White House also, but they're kind of in and out and they're more floaters in the process brought in at times to analyze certain aspects, obviously the legislative aspects, kind of give special interest group readings. You know, how they are going to react.

Tom Parsons spoke about another similar group.

> Well, there were top staff people from OMB and some economists. We had top staff people, lawyers from the Treasury and from the Council of Economic Advisors, and economists from the Council of Economic Advisors who were familiar with the programs, particularly the financing of them. You know, it's kind of like we assign that to the people who are familiar with it, and you say, will you develop something along these lines. And they come back to you and say, here's what we've got, and then the drafts go back and forth. And the Justice Department always had several good people because we were always talking about the law, and what can be done legally, and what cannot be done, particularly in this case.

This is not to say that it was always easy to put together a task group whose members were imaginative and could work easily with one another. Frank Miller talked about some of the difficulties he faced in creating a task group.

> This one was like mercury on this table. Every cabinet officer had a piece of the action. And because of that I remember calling literally every cabinet officer and saying: "Give me a bright guy. And I don't care if he's an assistant secretary. I'd rather he wouldn't be. I'd rather he'd be a GS-12 as long as he's bright." And I got a lot of turkeys. The cabinet officers did what would normally happen. They obviously wouldn't give you their indispensable bright guy because they need him. So I went through a series of

putting together a task group here where it took me a shakedown period of a
couple of months to get the right guys.

It is not easy to generalize about the activities of a working group because
their course of action depended so heavily on the subject matter with which they
were working and the phase of the decision-making process they were in at a
particular time. One group that Fred Winters was part of was doing a fair amount of
exploration in order to get a better sense of the parameters of a problem.

We had a couple of professors from major law schools. I mean it's a process
of trying to get the best minds that we could to look at the problem along the
way. And even before that we had a long string of meetings, meetings with
just interested people. We'd bring down a group of five or six people, and
we'd spend an afternoon talking about the problem, almost philosophizing.
We'd get into the problem itself, and also philosophizing. You know, what
do you think? What would happen if we did this? What do you think this
would result in? We'd throw out things, and we'd listen to just anybody that
we identified here that we thought would be helpful to us. Those were just
some of the things that the working group would do and would put together
to get input.

In another working group described by Mark Jensen, a basic decision had already
been made about the character of the program. Consequently, much of their discussion focused on the detailed decisions necessary to prepare a specific proposal and
the accompanying legislation.

In December of 1970 the decision had been made to go ahead with revenue
sharing as one of the six great goals. In that month we tried to develop what
we thought would be programmatically acceptable alternatives to six or
seven existing programs. We spent a month running out various formulae,
working out what we thought would be an equitable formula for distribution.
Alan Hampton is really the guy that headed the working group that did this.
Count in the people who did this, the OMB people working in this field,
and, obviously, the HEW people in the planning and management area and
in the secretary's office. Once we designed what we thought was an equita-
ble program, this was recommended to the president with the concurrence of
the secretary, OMB, and so forth.

The working group was not the only instrumentality the Domestic Council
used to develop policy. There were times when events moved too rapidly to permit
consultations and deliberations of this kind. There were also cases in which a single
staff man worked informally. Often proposals were developed in departments be-

fore being forwarded to the White House. Still, the working group was a device that was used repeatedly, and it had two distinct advantages. By allowing the Domestic Council staff to draw on OMB and the agencies for other members, the permanent Domestic Council staff could be kept lean. There was less need to duplicate departmental expertise within the White House when the skills of OMB and agency personnel could be brought to bear by including them in working groups. Further, the working group tied key departmental actors to program development. They had a chance to indicate their preferences; they knew what the difficult policy questions were; they knew what choices ultimately had been made by the president. All this considerably enhanced the chances of departmental support of a program when it was ultimately adopted.

The variations in the personal involvement of the president depended on the complexity and the political importance of the proposal. If the proposal was relatively simple and straightforward, submission of a single option paper and the president's reaction to it often marked the beginning and the end of presidential involvement. Bill Hunter, for example, spoke about a fairly standard series of options that had been given to the president by a task group he headed:

> *In this case, our recommendation was legislation, and a particular piece of legislation, and although that was his decision, the president was given a number of choices, from do nothing to attempt to do this administratively to submit a piece of legislation. These are the options given the president, you know, a, b, c from do nothing to submit legislation to varying shades in the middle, try to do it administratively, issue an executive order, and so forth, with the reasons pro and con on why we feel each of the options is bad or good. And then finally, after all the options, the recommended option, why you feel option b, let's say, is the best of four . . .*

In the case Hunter was describing the president accepted the recommendation of the working group, legislation was submitted, and ultimately a compromise bill was passed and signed by President Nixon. It was, Hunter concluded, "not as good as we would have liked to have, but it was certainly better than zero, which is where we were." The president's involvement in the decision-making was limited to his reaction to the original option paper. Once he had given his assent to submitting a piece of enabling legislation, there was no need to go back with further inquiries.

Major policy decisions were different. In such cases President Nixon was consulted relatively early in the process. Often he directed that further work be done, and would continue to be involved as the details of policy were worked out. David Archer recounted one meeting with President Nixon in which general approval was given to what the working group had accomplished to that point:

> *I guess that it was sometime in January that the president got the working group together and said, look, I'm going off to China, and when I come*

back I want, you know . . . He knew that we had been working on it, but he sat down and listened to what had been done up to that point, and he said, you know, when I get back, I want to be ready to do something. So we had about a three-week period in which you isolate yourself and you sit down and write.

Writing is always important to a White House staffer, but it was even more vital for a member of the Nixon Domestic Council staff. Richard Nixon had a strong preference for working from the written page. He liked to get away from the Oval Office so he could concentrate and think through a problem without interruption. In explaining to journalists why he made so many of his important decisions at Camp David, Mr. Nixon said:

I find that up here on top of a mountain it is easier for me to get on top of the job, to think in a generally relaxed way at times —although the work has been very intensive in these past few weeks, as it was before the other great decisions that have been made here —but also in a way in which one, if not interrupted either physically or personally or in any other way, can think objectively with perception about the problems one has to make a decision on.[7]

The "option paper" — in reality, a notebook two to three inches thick — fitted into this presidential working style. It was designed to give the president access to all the arguments, to present him with a wide range of choices, and to enable him to make his decisions in the solitude he preferred. One of the best descriptions of these option books was given by John Ehrlichman:

What we try to do on the substantive issues is to organize the materials with a brief cover page in which I try to summarize the nature of the issue, the nature of the controversy, so to speak, and refer the president to parts of the basic paper that I think will get him into the subject fastest and best. Then we present to him the range of alternatives. We give him the pros and cons and the views of those people, in and out of government, to whom we have had recourse. At the end we have a kind of "order blank" where he can indicate to us what his desires are with regard to next steps: either he's going to decide it now, and if so, what he decides, or if he wants additional information, additional work done, wants to talk about it, or whatever. Typically, he will take the notebook off to Camp David for the weekend, or wherever he happens to be. That's typical weekend reading. And he will get it back to me, generally, first thing Monday morning.[8]

Since these notebooks provided the basis for presidential decision, they had to be carefully written. Mindful of the need to give a dispassionate presentation of the views of all participants, Alan Hampton said his hardest problem was "to write Associated Press style rather than as a columnist." Even though the Domestic Council staffer had reached his own conclusion, he had to strive to present arguments in favor of all plausible options in order to preserve the final choice for the chief executive.

What kinds of questions went to President Nixon? They could be highly political, or potentially controversial, or basic policy questions. In the case of the Family Assistance Program, for example, there was the "ridge problem." This term refers to the point at which one runs into a disincentive to work because of payments one can receive for not working. The payment to any family is a combination of a "guarantee" and a "rate of reduction." If a family has no income at all, it receives an amount equal to the guarantee. If it has some income, then the payment it receives is reduced at a set rate. If the rate of reduction is too rapid, then there is a disincentive to work. The logical extension of this is that one can increase incentives to work by setting a low rate of reduction. Unfortunately, a low rate of reduction considerably increases the cost of the total program. One can design a program with maximum incentives to work at astronomic cost to the taxpayer; one can also design an inexpensive program with little incentive to work. The trick is to balance the two requirements.[9] Decisions of that kind went to the president.

Presidential reaction to the option books came in the form of inked commentary in the margins. Ward Norris explained this in discussing the kind of signals he got about presidential preferences:

> We produced this for the president, and when he went to Key Biscayne on Thanksgiving vacation, he read the whole damn book. . . . Here we talked about the thing as an issue in politics. We talked about its presentation, how it should be sold. And, for example, there's his writing. And this is what we said: "Hit the main issue in the State of the Union. Hit the main themes, and then follow up with cabinet things." And he said: "This sounds ok." So that was it. . . . Here's one that really attracted him. We're saying: "Let's solve the problems in the federal government first as an example." And he's saying: "A must. We can't show the states and the cities without setting an example. . . ." Here we get into organization. We're proposing taking one department plus pieces of another plus a regulatory agency, and creating a single department that can deal with these problems. He's saying: "Good idea." You know, we were kinda getting that kind of signal. He went through this thing, and that's how he got exposed and we got a sense of direction.

Since this program was to be a major theme in the State of the Union message, there was a good deal more direct interaction between Norris and the president in the weeks between Thanksgiving and the delivery of the message. "There were seven or eight meetings with him," Norris recalled, "which became more intense and more controversial the closer we got to February, when the message was sent down.'' This same pattern of intensive contact with the president prior to a major announcement was mentioned by David Archer:

The president saw the option paper after his return to Washington. His response was, here are the options — go back and put it in what you would call semifinal form. Then we went up to Camp David and spent three days finalizing it. This was a polishing session up there. The president personally was in on it, making the final, minor changes. Then the following night he went on TV to announce it.

The final stage in the process of presidential decision-making was a presentation to the public. This involved not only questions of when and how the presentation should be made, but also the preparation of separate messages for different groups. Kevin Daniels said he had been deeply involved in one such presentation:

The president accepted the recommendations. They were incorporated in the State of the Union message. What was decided was that in order to focus more congressional attention and more public attention on the issue, on the proposal, we would have a series of separate messages. The raw draft was written in the department. The Domestic Council — Flint and I — worked it over at this level. We got in what we wanted to say. Then, of course, (head speechwriter) Ray Price's people picked it up, put it into more coherent English, presidential prose, and it came out as a message. . . . This presentation was delivered by the president. It was a taped statement saying he was forwarding a message, what the message contained, and so forth. We wrote that here. Then I personally set up the press briefing, which brought the secretary and the assistant secretary over to the White House press room to be questioned about it. . . . Then once the message went up, actually before the message went up, we started congressional briefings. We brought them all down, both parties, and briefed them over in the Roosevelt Room on the proposals, on what we were trying to do . . .

As Daniels's conclusion implies, public announcement of a presidential decision did not end the activity of the Domestic Council. Once the president made his decision, the details of implementation (or following the progress of the legislation, if that had been the decision) were in the hands of Domestic Council staff members.

The principal concern of the Domestic Council staff in the decision-making process, then, was that of clarifying options. In their view, decisions about public policy were the most important activities of the president. They could best facilitate Mr. Nixon's choice-making by spending long hours turning up the information that would clarify his alternatives — and that was what they were doing.[10]

DETERMINING PRIORITIES

To Domestic Council staff members "determining priorities for the use of available resources" had a very concrete meaning. They were unlikely to use this phrase to refer to high-level discussion about reallocation of national priorities. To them, assignment of priorities meant, quite simply, making decisions. They were conscious of the need for choice-making because of their own experience. As Ralph Schmidt put it:

> *If seven of us have programs that we're pushing, and there are only funds for three, we all know that four of us are going to get shot down when the president makes his decisions.*

To them, the need for making hard decisions on priorities was something that was far better understood in the White House than either on Capitol Hill or in the agencies. Congressmen and cabinet members both had the luxury of advocating programs popular with their constituencies or departments. But at some point in the policy process, decisions had to be made that certain proposals were going to become part of the administration's legislative program, and other programs were not. This meant that someone was going to have to use that unpopular word, "No," and tell sponsors of certain proposals that they were not going to be backed by the administration.

Making decisions themselves was one of the activities that separated lower-ranking aides from leaders on the Council staff. This can be seen rather easily by taking the case of a recently appointed aide and contrasting it with that of an experienced leader who had developed an understanding of the kinds of decisions he could and could not make. Carl Baker's comments are typical of the novice.:

> *I don't sit down, dream up new programs, and then implement them myself. I sit down, try to dream up new programs, or new ways of doing existing things, and then send them up the organizational chart for discussion.*

Compare Baker's assumption that decisions should be made somewhere up the line with the comments of David Archer, one of the most experienced leaders on the staff.

> *This is the thing that every presidential aide grapples with. The problem when you get here, you think, is how the president makes decisions. The real problem is what decisions he should make. Let's say you have two departments differing with each other. Where are you going to get it decided? It's going to get decided by me — or if I think it's too tough, or the president should decide, by Ehrlichman — or, if not by Ehrlichman, by the president. So I've got to decide whether I should even tell Ehrlichman about it. So*

many decisions are made that way, without the president being talked to about them f.y.i. When you start this process, when you are new at it, you tend to think every decision should be made by the president. The longer you go along, the more you realize that can be a disservice to him because you can clutter up getting the real important decisions made.

Archer's comments at other points in this interview revealed that if he was uncertain about the president's preferences, or if he thought the president would want to make the decision himself, he would refer the question to the president through John Ehrlichman. Still, it is clear that David Archer—and the other leaders on the Domestic Council staff—were making a number of important decisions themselves.

There were limits to the staff authority to determine priorities. Any decision had to be consistent with the president's principles, and it had to fall within the substantive area being handled by the particular staff member. Many matters, however, fell within these limits. Frank Miller, for example, said that he was gathering information to determine whether previously submitted legislation should be altered or let stand.

I am directly in the process of meeting with all the outside groups to get from them what ideas they might have on how the legislative program could be improved. They've had twenty months to look at it; they've had time to talk about it. And there are areas where they think it can be improved. I'll also be working with the secretary of housing and urban development, because they've been asked if they have any modifications of the programs they'd like to recommend. We come to some agreement here. And I say here that I am responsible for getting HUD's views into the process, and making their views known to the president.

Now who was going to decide about the changes urged by either the interest groups or the department concerned? Miller continued:

I am also responsible for coordinating any changes, either major or minor, with OMB, and I and/or Ken Cole at that point would conclude that there are some changes here that the president should really get a chance to chop on—or that the changes are minor in nature, don't really change the president's principles, and go ahead and have HUD and our legislative people communicate these directly to the committees that are involved.

Ted Weber recounted some of his involvement with another piece of legislation that was being actively debated. His work in negotiating with interest groups, agencies, and senators meant that he was the man others in the White House asked whenever questions arose about this legislation.

As this unfolded we began to see in the Senate we were going to have a bill that was really the one written by this one interest group. We fought very hard. I spent hours in here with the interest group leaders, the HEW guy who was the focal point, and OMB people going over where were the areas of compromise. What can we do to gain your support? What can you do to gain our support? How can we come up with a bill that is mutually accepta-ble? What compromises are necessary, not just in programs, but what political compromises are necessary? And what we did, we kinda staked out what we thought were the basic principles that we stood for. I spent a year trying to rationalize pieces of the program so that those principles were somewhat not compromised. As it turned out, I was working as kind of the interface between the interest groups and HEW and OMB and the Con-gress. I just developed, you know, acceptable legislative compromises.

Weber's role as "interface between the interest groups and HEW and OMB and the Congress" meant that when the legislation reached the Senate floor he was neces-sarily involved in making some of the decisions about legislative tactics.

The authority of staff leaders to make decisions about priorities did not stop after a piece of legislation had been enacted into law. If anything, it increased after a basic policy decision had been made, because the basis of decision then became whether the proposed action was consistent with the policy that had been decided upon. Fred Winters explained his responsibilities in this situation:

So from that point on, I made a lot more decisions by myself or in concert with Budget, but still bucked a goodly sum of them up to Ehrlichman, and John bucked some of them to the president, and occasionally I'd meet with the president. But usually it was the sort of an issue that wasn't amenable to a conversation. Sometimes two contrasting cabinet officers would disagree and would clash, and the only way to preserve that relationship with the cabinet officers was to put it in an honest-to-God detailed option paper and say, "OK, boss, which way are we going?" Not that it made a hell of a lot of difference which way we went. But we can't sit here and say to a cabinet officer, "OK, you lose and you win." If he wants to appeal it and feels very strongly, we may say to him, "Mr. Secretary, is that worth his time?" You know . . . If he says, "Yeah, it is," then we'll stick it in.

It is apparent from descriptions such as these that Domestic Council staff members were deeply involved in decisions about a whole range of things: what legislation should be submitted to the Congress; how it could be advanced through the legislative labyrinth; and how it should be implemented after it was passed. There were no all-encompassing rules about which staff member made what kind of decisions, but that did seem to depend on the difficulty of the choice to be made and the importance of the person who raised the question in the first place. Few, if any, choices were being made by staff aides. A fair number of choices were being made by staff leaders, with the more difficult being made by Kenneth Cole or John Ehrlichman. The most perplexing problems, especially if they were being pressed by cabinet members, were apt to go to the president.

BACKSTOPPING THE PRESIDENT

One of the specific policy functions listed in the statement creating the Domestic Council was "providing rapid response to presidential needs for policy advice on pressing domestic issues." The inclusion of this assignment was paradoxical; it *seemed* not to fit. The other tasks — information-gathering, clarification of options, determining priorities, and monitoring agency activity—followed an orderly sequence. But there, in the middle of the list, was an explicit reference to emergency activities.

Staff leaders said in so many words that these fire-engine jobs didn't fit with their conception of the Domestic Council. When asked how much time she devoted to "backstopping the president by 'fire-engine' chores when answers are needed in a hurry," Mary Hickman said:

> *If you delete "when answers are needed in a hurry," a great deal of time. We're not here to provide quick answers. We're here to help solve problems.*

Bill Hunter acknowledged that he was spending more time on emergency chores than he wanted to, but at the same time he argued that the Domestic Council was intended to have a more programmatic focus.

> *I'm spending too much time on backstopping the president. Something goes wrong, and it's just gotta get fixed. But our conscious effort is just precisely not to do those kinds of things. That's what got the Domestic Council started . . . Let me digress for a moment. We came in here as aides to the president. It was really startling to us to understand that there literally had never been any kind of formal structure to deal with this kind of thing. It wasn't obvious why it hadn't existed so much as it was obvious that it had to exist now. So our first approach was to take some guys and say, "Ok, Kilgore, you handle labor; ok, Flint, you follow progress in school integration," and we were in the fire-putting-out business. We never had a chance to decide, to step back and decide what was important. So we got out of that business and created OMB with M for Management, and desperately tried to get out of the fire-fighting business and into the policy business. And we succeeded to some extent.*

In spite of the obvious desire of Domestic Council leaders for more orderly attention to fundamental questions, the data on time use show that the staff was spending
a fair amount of time on emergency activities. *Fire-engine chores are an inescap-
able part of life on the White House staff.*

Why should that be so? Part of the answer can be found in two of the factors
affecting administration behavior that we reviewed in the first chapter: the complexity of the political environment and the fixed political calendar. In combination,
they imply staying in touch with a large number of agencies, all of which must meet
recurring deadlines. Consequently, special effort is often needed just to get things
done on time. Often an emergency sequence is initiated by actions taken outside the
White House. For example, Fred Winters recalled a budget crisis faced by one of
the agencies with which he was dealing:

> *One of the things that came across my desk concerned the budget for the U.S.
> Information Agency. They are funded under the foreign appropriations
> bill, and they were severely cut back by the Congress after spending at the
> level of the previous fiscal year under a continuing resolution. They were in
> real trouble. They would have had to discharge many employees, cut the
> programming schedule away back, and so on. My recommendation was that
> the president find loose money among other international agencies, and bail
> them out. When this USIA budget matter came up, it took all my time for
> five or six days, and then the crisis was overcome, and that was it.*

As with other fire-engine tasks, this one monopolized time and attention but was of
limited duration.

Another example of seasonal employment for Domestic Council staff members comes from the election calendar. In the weeks immediately prior to the 1972
election, President Nixon gave dozens of speeches and surrogates campaigning in
his behalf delivered hundreds. Since the Domestic Council staff members knew
much more about the details of policy than most others around the White House,
they spent considerable time briefing others on the content of Nixon policies. Mary
Hickman spoke about what happened to her time as a result of the campaign:

> *In the six months preceding November 7, I'd say that backstopping the
> president occupied a very substantial portion of my time. The supply of
> information, updating information was . . . In other words, at that point the
> president had the opportunity, indeed, the duty to advise America what his
> record was and where we were, so I was constantly updating the statistics,
> and showing what we had done for farm income, for giving the farmer a fair
> share of American prosperity, where we were with respect to the commodity
> programs, and so on.*

Once the election was over, of course, this campaign-specific activity ended. As with the budget example above, the campaign activity was intense but completely removed from the agenda immediately after the election.

A further reason why emergency chores bulk so large in the White House is that there are certain kinds of issues that seem to generate such activity. Some activities directly touch the lives of a great many people. Other matters cannot be dealt with routinely because there is not yet a settled governmental policy. Tom Parsons, for example, pointed out:

> *Given the nature of the issues I deal with, I spend a great deal of time on fire-engine chores. Busing, for example, can become a crisis issue with very little notice.*

Bill Hunter made a parallel comment:

> *Putting out fires day by day would probably be 40 percent of the time, I would say. There are a lot of discrete problems, particularly in the areas that are just emerging. The bureaucracy . . . It is not a routine thing yet on a lot of these problems. The Congress is red hot on this issue. There were 948 environmental bills, I think, submitted in the 92nd Congress. And there are lots of fires. So that's probably half of the time spent just on discrete problems.*

Busing, of course, touches the lives of many citizens, and pollution control presents many of the problems of emerging issues. Since these types of issues demonstrably call for emergency responses from time to time, it follows that the Domestic Council could not have expected to escape such chores. For the issues that consumed most of the time of the Domestic Council staff (social welfare, followed by economic management and civil liberties in that order) were just those that touched many lives. And the not-yet-settled issues were just those that were likely to be referred to the White House for resolution.

COLLECTING INFORMATION

The proportion of staff time devoted to gathering information was modest. Most of the staff members had too many other demands on their time to permit any substantial allocation to the assembly of data and reflection about future events. That is not to say, of course, that the staff was operating without information at hand. Tom Parsons drew an important distinction:

> *Directly, we spend very little time on this, but we pull a lot of strings to make sure that this gets done. We try to sit down with the people who are staffed up to do that sort of thing. The Council of Economic Advisors, the*

Office of Science and Technology, the Office of Management and Budget plus the bureaucracies and the program development types out there all do a lot of this sort of thing.

Parsons went ahead to speak about one study for which he had been responsible.

There's a little gray book called the economic impact of population growth. When I first came here, one of the first things we did was to sit down with the chairman of the Council of Economic Advisors and say everyone in the federal government has a different version of what the economic impact of population growth is. You're the only one with neutral credibility in the area of economics to be able to wrestle all these competing numbers to the mat, have everybody agree on the underlying bases for them, and to make projections that are at least comparable in that they start from the same kind of denominator. So they did that, and I think it's a very useful function. We weren't in on the working group that made these projections, but there were a lot of man hours spent because we got them started.

This suggests that the Domestic Council staff recognized the need for information full well. Lacking the time to gather the intelligence themselves, they delegated the task to others.[11]

Much information was being absorbed by this staff. Some of this would have been inevitable, given the political environment within which the Domestic Council staff was situated. But beyond that, staff members regarded the acquisition of information as an important activity. Alan Hampton spoke at considerable length about the various information sources with which he was in regular contact.

Each assistant director has within his area certain antennae that operate. One is people in the agencies that are what I call early warning of problems that are upcoming as well as opportunities. And each one of us has three or four relatively influential people in the agencies that we contact on a regular basis, daily. . . . Another one, and this is one that a lot of people miss, we talk to a fantastic range of people. . . . When we're out, maybe a speech in California, we'll talk to educators pro and con. And there are a lot of ideas that get popped into the system at this level. . . . Another thing, frankly, is just the old yellow pad, working on things that you as an individual think ought to be done, improvements that ought to be made, both in the policy and the process. Another thing that I've gotten close to is OMB and the budget business, and I've found that if you do it right, the Domestic Council has to be the vehicle through which the departments and OMB fight their budget battles.

The intelligence gathered in this way is better visualized as a substantial number of policy cues than any formal report. Those cues, of course, had to be brought to bear on substantive matters, but the staffers knew whose attention should be called to the items of information they picked up. The longer they gleaned bits of intelligence in this way, the better they learned just what kind of information could be obtained from each source. That was important because the Domestic Council staff members needed facts to do their own jobs. Nancy Schuster pointed this out:

> *As a day-to-day function, it's clear that I cannot work in the area of taxes without knowing where we're going to be next year, two years from now, ten years from now. I just have to have some projections on what the costs of our programs are likely to be, and what our expected revenue will be given our tax rates and various states of the economy.*

Mutual needs for information involved the group and its environment in a symbiotic relationship. Agencies, interest groups, politicians, and other actors outside the White House needed to get views and facts into the decision-making process; the Domestic Council staff needed information in order to do its job. Hence much information was passed along, and, to the extent that process improved the staff's judgment about what sources were able to supply what kinds of intelligence, they were able to bring better information to bear on their own activities.

Any discussion of the intelligence function of the Domestic Council staff requires further specification as to who was doing what. Many staff members weren't spending too much time making long-range projections because there was one shop with that specific responsibility. This shop, which came closest to making long-range forecasts on national needs, was spending much of its time integrating work done by others, and occasionally initiating a long-range study others had not undertaken.

The integrative aspects commanded more of their attention.[12] It is hard to give any simple description to this integration. Some of the efforts were straightforward ties between related substantive programs.

> *For example, one of the main concerns of older people is crime. So we've got to make sure that whoever is handling crime is plugged in with the people dealing with the problems of the aged.*

Other integrative activities were far more complex. This shop had the primary responsibility for liaison with the Office of Management and Budget and for the development of revenue sharing, as well as for bringing materials together for the State of the Union message and preparing an overview of first-term accomplishments. These responsibilities blended into planning in a very real sense. As Kevin Daniels explained:

We worked with a multiyear time horizon, and tried to work out the issues that we wanted to put forward at any particular time.

Not surprisingly, the time frame for any "long-range" planning of which Domestic Council staffers spoke resulted from the political calendar. Messages to Congress had to be ready by the "message season" early in the year. And Kevin Daniels pointed to *the* deadline that commands the attention of all officeholders when he remarked that during the first term,

> . . . *the time horizon was four years. We wanted to have things accomplished at the time our report was going to be marked.*

In view of all this it would be inaccurate to think of the Domestic Council as an intelligence unit, or one much concerned with affairs that ran longer than the length of an administration. Staff members were making use of information from a variety of sources, but most of the detailed estimates came from agencies that were better staffed for the preparation of such analyses.

MONITORING AGENCY ACTIVITY

Domestic Council staff members were spending the least amount of time keeping close tabs on day-to-day agency activity. There were a number of possible reasons for this. First, any real surveillance would require the intimate acquaintance with agency activity that normally takes years to acquire. Second, oversight of routine matters was formally assigned to the Office of Management and Budget. Third, most agency activity follows established patterns and doesn't need to come to White House attention. But even with those activities that did bear on the programs of the president, the Domestic Council staff was just too small to carry on any very active surveillance. Dan Bailey explained his situation quite directly:

> *Bill and I are all there are in this area . . . Obviously, with only two people, we don't sit here and monitor all the research that is going on in the entire Department of Defense, and the National Institutes of Health, and under the sponsorship of the National Science Foundation or the Office of Science and Technology . . .*

In the time available to them Domestic Council staff members could find out a few things about what was going on in a few agencies.

Most of the oversight of the agencies by the staff took two forms: that growing out of routine reports and liaison, and that found necessary to get specific programs moving. Some of the routine contacts with the agencies were described by Scott Manning in talking about his own job.

> *I get some mail to answer. But more importantly, I work closely with the departments and with OMB at the same time. When the departments have to submit reports to Congress, I'm the one who has to observe them. . . . And on my own recently, I've had some meetings with my agencies just so I won't be surprised.*

Manning was one of the aides who did spend a great deal of time monitoring agency activity. His fund of information gathered from meetings with agency personnel, sitting through their budget hearings, and reading their reports was doubtless superior to that of colleagues whose attention was drawn elsewhere by other responsibilities. A more typical liaison was that discussed by Lane Redman:

> *Education is likely to be the responsibility of a single department, in the normal course of events, HEW. In that situation the activity is much more one of maintaining liaison with the secretary and the assistant secretary and keeping tabs on developments, i.e., here's an alternative or an option . . . In the sense that there may be certain legal problems, of course bringing those aspects here to the attention of the Office of Legal Counsel, to Justice, and sometimes to outside people. . . . I mention this only because it concerns a particular department. It is a kind of one-on-one operation; it tends not to be a coordination among various players.*

Here the posture was one of helpful liaison. If matters that merited being passed along to others were brought to the staff member's attention, he would do so. But there was no special effort to seek out information about policies to which the department did not choose to draw his attention.

The other type of oversight concerned specific programs. This type of contact was most likely to occur when the policy process had led to a new program, and attention had turned to the question of implementation. There was, for example, concern about aid for returning veterans. An inquiry was sent to the agencies asking them to identify areas where there could be a quick impact, where existing resources could be used, and where proposed programs would be consistent with the president's philosophy. One suggestion was that existing benefit programs were not being fully used because some veterans were unaware of them. A simple mailing to veterans could tell them what benefits they were entitled to, and how to contact the appropriate agency close to the area where they were residing. Pat Thornburg spoke about his involvement in that effort:

> *We spent the next three or four months deciding just how to do this. This*

took quite a bit of coordination. The Veterans' Administration administered most of the benefit programs; the Defense Department had the best list of discharged servicemen; the Postal Service had to be involved because of the increased work load. . . . I acted as a go-between with these agencies. It was my job to identify tasks that had to be done, to determine what resources should be put together, and so on.

The mailing was sent out in August, and reply cards came back to a central point the following month. Thereafter Thornburg's personal activity dropped off rapidly. As he explained it:

We define areas where action should be taken, and get policy decisions made. Then, to the extent that we have to, we monitor agencies to make sure that action is being taken, and then we get out. Our job is to catalyze action.

There were times, of course, when action was not forthcoming, or at least not forthcoming rapidly enough to satisfy the president. Just that happened in an effort to expand the food stamp program for needy families. Frank Miller spoke about what took place then:

At that point, although OMB normally has the management and prodding function, I got into that — going to meetings, and sending out memoranda to anybody whose job it was to make some progress on that food stamp thing. It didn't happen, because there was a bureaucratic process of regulations and sign-offs and this sort of thing, and it wasn't happening. And we ended up calling in the procurement officers and saying, "I don't care whether it's happened or not, or whether those regs are there. You know they're coming. So start telling everybody that this is what we want to happen." In effect, we started cutting some red tape, and I got into a management role that I normally or theoretically would not perform. We just kept hammering and hammering on enough people until it finally eked its way out into the bureaucracy and some things started to happen.

Such reports make it clear that occasionally Domestic Council staff members were closely involved with particular programs. That contact, though, tended to be short-lived. It ended as soon as the program appeared to be proceeding satisfactorily, or credit had been won, or it was no longer controversial, or—most likely—the staff member's attention returned to some higher-priority Domestic Council task. Consequently, neither the involvement with particular programs nor the liaison already discussed brought anything approaching full information to the Domestic Council. Some staff members had good information about certain programs within their purview, but this was far short of a comprehensive oversight of the executive branch.

REVENUE SHARING

Although the responsibilities of the president and the Domestic Council were quite different, each needed the other. The president needed a Domestic Council (or its functional equivalent) to do the detailed work in policy development, and the Council looked to the president for intervention at crucial times in the process to make basic decisions. A review of the development of revenue sharing in the Nixon administration provides some sense of the continuing interaction between the president and the Domestic Council. No single example, of course, is "typical" of the wide variety of undertakings by an administration, and no one should think of revenue sharing as revealing all about the Nixon administration. This example does, however, help to underscore some of the rhythms of policy development and the roles played by the president and the Council.

The idea of revenue sharing had been discussed for some years by a number of political leaders. The basic point was that while the responsibilities of state and local governments to provide services had been growing rapidly the federal government had preempted the most lucrative tax resources. Since financially anemic governments could not be responsive governments, the argument ran, the federal government ought to share some of its more plentiful revenues. This theme had been supported throughout the sixties by some important Democrats and Republicans, but the idea had not won presidential acceptance. That was to come with Richard Nixon in the White House.

The beginning of a formal Nixon position on revenue sharing came in late November, 1968, with a report by the president-elect's Intergovernmental Fiscal Relations Task Force. This group strongly endorsed the notion, not only for the fiscal reasons already mentioned, but also as a way of returning some political power to the subfederal levels of government. They advocated sharing one-half of 1 percent of the individual income tax revenues, some $1.75 billion, with state and local governments.

In April, 1969, President Nixon appointed an interagency committee to develop a report on revenue sharing. Although the Domestic Council was not yet in existence, the membership of this committee resembled the working groups the Council was later to employ. It was chaired by then Presidential Counselor Arthur Burns, and in his absence it was led by Murray Weidenbaum, an economist who had become assistant secretary of the treasury with special responsibilities for revenue sharing. The other members came from the vice president's office, the White House, the Office of Management and Budget, and the Council of Economic Advisors. This committee worked through May and June to prepare a report that called for: (1) an automatic distribution of a fixed proportion of the federal income tax revenues; (2) fair shares of this money to both the state and local governments; (3) no restrictions on the use of these funds by subfederal government; and (4) inclusion of all general-purpose local governments. Each of these goals was to be implemented by formulas included in the legislation. These four points were agreed to in a meeting on July 8, 1969, between President Nixon and a group of governors, mayors, and county officials. The next day the Revenue Sharing Committee met again to follow up and arrange to have legislation drafted.

The Treasury Department sent draft legislation to the White House in early August. There it received immediate attention. In his television address on August 8 presenting the Family Assistance Program, President Nixon said:

> For a third of a century, power and responsibility have flowed toward Washington, and Washington has taken for its own the best sources of revenue. We intend to reverse this tide, and to turn back to the states a greater measure of responsibility —not as a way of avoiding problems, but as a better way of solving problems.
>
> Along with this would go a share of federal revenues. I shall propose to the Congress next week that a set portion of the revenues from federal income taxes be remitted directly to the states, with a minimum of federal restrictions on how these dollars are to be used, and with a requirement that a percentage of them be channeled through for the use of local governments.

Five days later the president sent a special message to Congress calling for a first-year payment of $500 million, building to a payment of $5 billion by 1976. Legislation to that end was introduced in both the House and the Senate on September 23.

The Congress was not quick to act on the matter, and the next months were devoted to eliciting public support. State and local officials were among those whose active backing was most eagerly sought. Speeches were given to city managers, the Annual Congress of Cities, members of the Oregon legislature, Florida municipal finance officers, and other similar groups. These officeholders were willing to help. They knew the dimensions of their financial problems, and that knowledge, once communicated, was to be important in convincing congressmen that subfederal governments urgently needed legislative relief. On April 16, 1970, a joint press conference was held in behalf of revenue sharing by the official associations of the governors, mayors, cities, legislative leaders, counties, and city managers. In mid-May state and local organizations sent out a strategy manual on revenue sharing, and Governor Buford Ellington of Tennessee sent along a covering letter calling for an "all-out push from the states at this time to get hearings underway."

Although it was by now obvious that it was going to be difficult to obtain congressional approval, the efforts continued. On June 24 President Nixon sent a memorandum to senior administration officials stating that "revenue sharing is the financial heart of the New Federalism," and the president continued his advocacy in a "regional cabinet meeting" attended by several governors in Louisville, Kentucky, on July 14, 1970. At the same time the Domestic Council staff was holding three-hour-long meetings for a two-week period to review all departmental suggestions for the coming year's legislative program. One of their recommendations was that revenue sharing should be a high priority item. At budget and policy review meetings held at San Clemente at the end of July, the president decided that revenue sharing would be a high priority issue in his program for fiscal year 1972. During the following three months, Treasury, OMB, and White House personnel continued to meet with state and local officials to discuss means of promoting revenue sharing.

Presidential attention returned to revenue sharing in early November. In his talks with citizens and officials during the 1970 campaign, the president had sensed an increasing frustration with the incapacity of government. He felt that major change was needed if the people were to feel that government was both responsive and effective, and that revenue sharing might be a way to enable local governments to do more to meet urgent needs. Consequently, Mr. Nixon directed that attention be given to the possibility of a vastly expanded revenue sharing program, perhaps one that would end categorical grants and use the funds for a program of general revenue sharing.

The Domestic Council staff began work on it at once. At a meeting on November 9, 1970, the senior staff discussed a much expanded program, and OMB was asked to prepare a list of programs that could be included if revenue sharing were begun at the $30 billion level. The next day a Domestic Council staff paper was prepared listing all categorical grant programs and suggesting a set of criteria that might be used to determine which grant programs should be maintained and converted into revenue sharing. The basic test posed was whether there was a true federal question involved in any given program. The paper argued that in the past many programs that were properly matters to be addressed by state and local governments had been assumed by the federal government. Four criteria were proposed to determine the existence of a federal question: (1) Is there a need for national consistency in the program? (2) Is the program one that could not be accomplished without federal participation and sponsorship? (3) Does federal action result in demonstrably greater effectiveness? (4) Is the program sufficiently novel to require the cutting edge of federal attention? This staff paper formed the basis for discussion with the president while he was flying to Europe for President de Gaulle's funeral. President Nixon decided that not all categorical grant programs should be included, but that judicious selection should be made employing these criteria.

The next few weeks were marked by intensive work by several parties. The Treasury and OMB both submitted memorandums to the White House discussing sharing formulas, criteria for selection of programs that might be included, and some background on grant programs that might be included. The president met with leaders of the National Association of County Officials, and first President Nixon, and then Vice President Agnew, met with leaders of the Republican Governors' Association. Assistant Treasury Secretary Weidenbaum met with state and local officials in Las Vegas on November 20, and again in Atlanta on December 6. At the last meeting agreement was reached on a pass-through formula to determine how much would go to local governments, and a unanimous joint statement endorsing the program was distributed to the press. The Domestic Council staff continued their work, both collectively and individually. At a meeting in his office on December 7, John Ehrlichman asked that a presentation be prepared for the president on the pros and cons of specific proposals under discussion.

A presentation on large-scale conversion of grant programs to revenue sharing took place in the president's Executive Office Building office on December 12. In addition to the president, this meeting was attended by his principal economic advisors — George Shultz and Caspar Weinberger of OMB and Paul McCracken of the Council of Economic Advisors — and John Ehrlichman and Edwin Harper of the Domestic Council staff. The president directed that the same presentation be made to a much larger group. This meeting took place three days later in the Cabinet Room, with Mr. Nixon joining the discussion after the presentation. There it developed that in a number of key areas — elementary and secondary education, community development, transportation, law enforcement, and manpower — cabinet members had been working independently toward a block grant approach. The president indicated that he was not satisfied with block grants. He had advocated them years before, but he now felt they didn't go far enough, and that they were too restrictive in their requirements for prior presidential approval. In closing, he asked each person to prepare a memorandum as if he had to make the final decision. These memorandums were gathered into a notebook given to Mr. Nixon on December 19.

On January 3, 1971, at San Clemente, the president decided to go ahead with a general revenue sharing program at the $5 billion level and an additional $11.4 billion program of special revenue sharing. The latter would consolidate a number of existing federal programs into six broad programs toward which the cabinet members had already begun working. The appropriations were to reflect the cost of the existing programs plus an additional billion dollars to reflect national priorities and insure that state and local governments would not get less under special revenue sharing than under existing programs. During the next ten days Domestic Council and OMB staff reviewed a list of grant programs to look for any technical problems that might exist, and on January 12 the president made his final decision about programs to be included in the revenue sharing package.

It was now time to "go public" with the revenue sharing proposals. On January 22 this was done most visibly in the president's State of the Union message, in which revenue sharing was accented as one of the president's "Six Great Goals"; on February 4, in a message on general revenue sharing; and during March in messages on each of the special revenue sharing programs. At the same time Domestic Council staff members were holding extensive briefings for congressmen, and administration leaders were addressing state and local leaders on every possible occasion. The president spoke to the National Governors Conference; the vice president traveled around the country; Assistant Treasury Secretary Weidenbaum continued his meetings with a now extensive network of state and local officials.

The support by subfederal officials created a political climate that made passage of general revenue sharing possible,[13] but a protracted effort was still necessary. Quite beyond the difficulties of devising a strategy to deal with an opposition Congress, revenue sharing entailed three great questions that had concerned the Constitutional Convention of 1787: the proper location of the power of the purse, the power of the federal government versus that of subfederal jurisdictions, and the large states versus the small states. Each of these matters had to be dealt with in both the House and the Senate.

The legislation was referred to the House Ways and Means Committee, where it at first faced opposition by the powerful chairman, Wilbur Mills. Congressman Mills called it "a bad and dangerous proposal" and said that he intended to use hearings to kill the bill. Conversations with state and local officials, however, led Mills to the conclusion that there was a genuine local financial crisis, and he announced his support of a bill that would allow two-thirds of the money to reach the municipal and county level. His committee reported such a measure in April, 1972. There was still considerable opposition to the bill, and the Rules Committee barely (by a vote of 8 to 6) granted a closed rule, which meant that no amendments would be in order. During the floor debate in June, important opponents voiced basic objections. Chairman George Mahon of the Appropriations Committee argued that funding ought to pass through his committee as part of the annual appropriations cycle, and not be allocated automatically by a bill coming from Ways and Means. Congressmen John Byrnes and Sam Gibbons both felt the federal government ought to retain the right to stipulate how money should be spent rather than ceding the privilege to subfederal jurisdictions. Many congressmen from small states objected to the distribution formula, which emphasized large urban populations as well as favoring states that had income taxes. But the Democratic and Republican floor leaders backed passage, and when the crucial vote came on a technical parliamentary motion (to invoke the previous question to vote on the closed rule), Republicans voted 2 to 1 in favor, Northern Democrats 13 to 10 in favor, and Southern Democrats 3 to 1 against. The vote was relatively narrow (223 to 185), but affirmative.

The Senate acted more swiftly. The Finance Committee chose a formula favoring the smaller, less wealthy states (which have greater representation in the upper chamber), then added $1 billion in social services, so only four states would receive less than under the House-approved formula. The floor debate in September echoed some of the points made in the House. Appropriations Chairman John McClellan also argued that all funding should be left in his committee's jurisdiction, and some large-state senators, such as Robert Taft of Ohio, objected to a formula that would result "in a serious net loss to a great many states, and, particularly, to many of our large cities." But on September 12 the Senate voted 64 to 20 in favor, with the limited opposition coming from Southern Democrats and a few senators from the large states disadvantaged by the distribution formula. As it turned out, the Conference Committee protected the interests of both large and small states by allowing each state to choose the formula that allocated it the most money. Final approval of this compromise came in mid-October.

There was no question of a veto of a measure so eagerly sought by the administration. The only remaining choice was the location of the signing ceremony, and this was another decision made by the president. Mr. Nixon saw revenue sharing as an historic turning point, a measure that could have considerable impact on the federal system itself. Consequently, he chose to go to Philadelphia, where the original decisions about the federal system had been made. So on the afternoon of October 20, 1972, eight hundred dignitaries gathered at Independence Hall. In brief remarks before his signature completed the long legislative process, Richard Nixon spoke of his hopes for revenue sharing:

> *What America wants today, at the state level, at the city level, and at the county level, and I believe at the federal level, is not bigger government, but better government, and that is what this is all about. And so I would hope that each mayor, and each governor, and each county official would go back to his community, or his state or hers, with this dedication in mind: that these funds will be used for the needs of the people, that they will mean better schools and better hospitals and better police forces . . .*

By giving state and local officials the financial capability to act, the Nixon administration hoped to show its ability to respond to local needs and problems.

SUMMARY

Domestic Council staff work was concentrated on clarifying choices to be made by the president, and making the much larger number of decisions that were not important enough to be referred to the chief executive. Emergency activities, "fire-fighting," were also an important part of the staff responsibilities. In the time remaining to them, some effort was devoted to collecting information and monitoring agency activity.

Viewed in the larger context of the development of revenue sharing, the efforts of the Domestic Council staff, however vital, were only one portion of a complex policy-making process. Before the Nixon administration even took office, there had been an incubation period during which the proposal gained public support. Continuing responsibility for drafting proposals and staying in touch with potential supporters was lodged in a department (Treasury) with relevant expertise. The Domestic Council coordinated the efforts of the many actors and proposals coming from a number of sources, but the president himself also took part from time to time, affirming some decisions, vetoing others, and sometimes changing the scope of the whole enterprise. The support of congressional leaders had to be won. In this case, it meant cooperating with state and local leaders throughout the country in a three-year lobbying campaign. And finally, the president's signature only began the program. With revenue sharing, as with all other new programs, it would be some time before there would be much good evidence about how it was working in practice.

NOTES

[1] The specific policy functions listed by the president may be found on page 20.

[2] For an explanation of the measurement of time use by activity, see Appendix A4.1.

[3] For an explanation of the analysis of time use by issue area, see Appendix A4.2.

[4] This is in part a consequence of the number of people involved. Of the 18 persons for whom time use data are available, 15 were spending at least "a fair amount" of time on social benefits, and 12 were spending that much time on economic management. Since the populations are nearly the same, the means could not vary much.

[5] There were some differences between these two areas, but they can be treated together here because most of the activity was centered in the same shop.

[6] For a detailed account of the Family Assistance Plan see Daniel P. Moynihan, *The Politics of a Guaranteed Income: The Nixon Administration and the Family Assistance Plan* (New York: Random House, 1973).

[7] *Washington Post*, November 28, 1972, p. A10.

[8] Frank Cormier, "Nixon's Decision Process: He's Not an 'Agonizer,'" *Washington Star-News*, November 13, 1972, p. D–20.

[9] For a lucid discussion of this problem, see David N. Kershaw, "A Negative Income Tax Experiment," *Scientific American*, October, 1972, pp. 19–25.

[10] There is a possibility that staff members may have overemphasized their role in decision-making because they did think it was so important. I am inclined to discount this possibility for two reasons. First, the respondents were asked about their time use and/or activities at three separate points in the interview, which provides a good check on the validity of the data. Second, the same motivation that might lead them to overemphasize that part of their jobs would also lead them to work hard on those projects. I think the motivation was genuine, and so was the effort.

[11] If the analysis was being delegated to others, some of the decision was being delegated as well. Recall what we learned in Chapter 2 about the importance of expertise as a base of power within the group, and Pat Thornburg's comment in Chapter 3 about departmental ability to influence the Domestic Council by providing the facts to be considered.

[12] We have already seen, in Chapter 2, how this shop was important in providing inter-shop communication among staff members.

[13] The failure of the 92nd Congress to enact special revenue sharing is another story. A number of congressional and agency leaders were not so enthusiastic about special revenue

sharing, and there was much less support for it by state and local officials. Whereas general revenue sharing meant unencumbered new money to local officials, special revenue sharing meant they would have to decide whether or not to continue some existing programs. This latter task meant saying no to various groups, and local officials preferred keeping this politically unpopular chore on the federal level.

Chapter 5

A Limited Assessment

The exact pattern of activity we have reviewed came to an end shortly after the 1972 election. Before Richard Nixon began his second term, Kenneth Cole had succeeded John Ehrlichman as executive director of the Domestic Council, and a reduction in the size of the Council staff was announced. Then, of course, there was a period of considerable flux among the president's senior advisors beginning with the Watergate-connected resignations of H. R. Haldeman and John Ehrlichman. The patterns of influence around the president were, to put it mildly, unsettled during this period.

Since they were responsible for things that had to be done, Watergate crisis or no, the Domestic Council staff was less affected than many other elements of the Nixon White House. They continued with their responsibilities, and Kenneth Cole was promoted to assistant to the president for domestic affairs in January, 1974. Many of the habits formed by the Council staff during the first Nixon term doubtless influenced their behavior during the rest of Mr. Nixon's tenure in the White House. Still, it would be well to regard the first-term pattern as only an approximate guide to the second-term activity of the Council staff.

While we don't know what future presidents will do, it is clear that Gerald Ford and his successors have to deal with the same problems that confronted Richard Nixon and his Domestic Council. How can a staff be recruited and organized to deal with domestic policy? What patterns of communication and influence will develop within the staff, and how will staff views be communicated to the chief executive? How can the staff deal with the complex political environment in which they are situated? How can they adequately convey the wishes and views of other actors to the president and his senior advisors, and how can they faithfully represent the president's wishes to others? How can the choices implicit in presidential decisions best be clarified so the president knows what he is deciding and when? How can a balance best be maintained between orderly decision-making and emergency activities, or between short-range decisions that must be made and

111

long-range planning that is certainly desirable? These have been problems confronting White House staffs for some time, and they will continue to be in the future.

But now we ought to turn from a description of how the Nixon Domestic Council staff did these jobs to some questions — within the limits of the data available — about how well they carried out their overall responsibilities. Specifically, we want to ask three questions. First, *how well did the Domestic Council staff serve the needs of this president*? Second, *how well did it serve the interests of the voters*? Third, *how well did it serve the needs of the presidency*?

THE NEEDS OF RICHARD NIXON

Of all our presidents, Richard Nixon is one of the most puzzling. He had the gifts to undertake foreign initiatives that restructured international relationships in fundamental ways, and he proposed some not unimportant changes in domestic policy as well. Yet he also concealed knowledge of criminal activities from legal authorities for over two years, and thereby utterly destroyed his capacity to lead. It is never easy to discern the personal needs that lie behind a behavior pattern, but in the Nixon case the behavior pattern that combined high achievement with tragic failure is itself a paradox.

There are two facets of the Nixon personality that may have been related to this combination of success and failure, and that were certainly associated with the president's work habits. Richard Nixon was genuinely intelligent, and profoundly mistrustful. The former characteristic was well described in Theodore White's books about the 1968 and 1972 campaigns, and the latter was unmistakably revealed in the Watergate transcripts.

Richard Nixon's mind was capacious; he fairly drank in facts. In 1967, Theodore White found:

> . . . *a new view of the Nixon personality — in which the trait that was uppermost was a voracious, almost insatiable curiosity of mind, a hunger to know, to learn, to find out how things work, to understand and explore in detail.*[1]

After Mr. Nixon had completed a term in the White House, White wrote:

> *The range of Richard Nixon's mind was astonishing — it reached from the problems of Singapore to the exports of Japan, to the minutiae of Southern California politics, to the cost factors in political publicity, to the sequence of railroad towns in Ohio — just which towns lay north or south of Lima, Ohio, for example, and what people made there. . . . Nixon had the courage to face facts even when they did not fit together. In conversation, his*

mind could go, zip, from what appeared to be a covering banality to the
most precise exposition of sustaining and contradictory facts.[2]

Curiosity was not the only motive, though. There was also a need for order. If
Richard Nixon was to use these facts, if he was to bring them to bear on a decision,
he had to have time to arrange them in his own fashion. This could not be a rushed
process; his mind had to have time to order the facts in his own way. Alexander
Haig, Mr. Nixon's second-term chief of staff, observed:

> *The President thinks very, very carefully before he makes a decision. He*
> *does it in the most methodical, meticulous and unraveled way. And once he*
> *makes a decision, he agonizes even less.*[3]

Turning from the way Richard Nixon thought about things to the way he
related to other persons reveals very different motives. Veteran politicians were
startled to discover that lists of enemies were circulated in the Nixon White House,
but the comments Mr. Nixon made about his own colleagues told even more about
the hostility he harbored. President Nixon said that Herbert Klein, who had faithfully supported him for more than two decades, "didn't have his head screwed on
right." Of Secretary of the Treasury George Shultz, he complained, "I didn't send
him over there to be a candy ass." When discussing William Rehnquist, whom he
shortly afterward elevated to the Supreme Court, the president recalled:

> *. . . Nobody follows up on a God damn thing. We've got to follow up on this*
> *thing; however, we had that meeting. You remember the meeting we had*
> *when I told that group of clowns we had around there. Renchburg and that*
> *group. What's his name?*

One should be cautious in drawing inferences from these comments. If we had
access to unvarnished statements from other political leaders, they might be similar.
We know that a need for power and a lack of need for personal friendship (affilia-
tion) is a combination of motives found in many politicians.[4] Even so, the depth of
suspicion and hostility toward Mr. Nixon's own supporters is remarkable.

Now, how was this combination of needs — a desire for facts, a passion for
order, a mistrust of others, and a determination to hold power himself — related to
his work habits? The simplest answer is that the paper flow in the White House
provided all the information that Mr. Nixon wanted while minimizing the personal
contact he found more difficult. There is much about the way Richard Nixon
worked as president that shows a reliance on reading and relatively little contact
with other persons. In a March, 1973, conversation with Theodore White, Mr.
Nixon explained his thoughts on a desirable White House structure:

> *I'm getting the government reorganized in such a way that the President can*

> *spend his time on the most important things . . . and we'll see how success-*
> *fully we can do that. My disposition is to see that the President's time is not*
> *frittered away. I've found a way to do that. I'm a reader, not a buller. Most*
> *of the boys at the Law School had long bull sessions about their cases. I*
> *studied my cases alone. The space committee, the medical committee, the*
> *science committee —if they give me a paper, I'll read it.*[5]

This statement was remarkable, both for the president's emphasis on reading and for the vague reference to "the space committee, the medical committee, (and) the science committee." At the time, there was one Domestic Council staffer who was coordinating health policy, and the Office of Science and Technology had been abolished. Mr. Nixon apparently did not know much about the White House administrative structure beyond his immediate circle.

The group of persons reporting directly to the president was limited to the few he trusted. Alexander Butterfield, a deputy to H. R. Haldeman, testified that 60 percent of the time that the president spent with any staff member in 1972 was spent with his chief of staff, and that for 90 percent of that time they were alone.[6] Furthermore, the president often sought physical isolation and greater serenity when addressing himself to a problem. He would retreat from the Oval Office to the Executive Office Building. Whenever possible, he wanted to get even farther away: Camp David, Key Biscayne, or San Clemente.

It follows that for White House staff to get Richard Nixon's attention, they had to put their arguments on paper and have them transmitted through a person trusted by the president. The thick option books that went from the Domestic Council staff through John Ehrlichman fitted this pattern very nicely. Everything was written down; all the arguments were summarized; the president could read as much or as little as he chose. Mr. Nixon could take the books when he left the White House and pore over them in isolated surroundings. Here there were no raised voices, no challenges to his propriety or authority; only the facts and supporting arguments on neatly typed paper. In this setting Richard Nixon was in full control. He had the facts before him, and the serenity to digest those bits of information. Since the Domestic Council was able to develop a work style that accorded with President Nixon's personal needs, they were able to serve their chief executive. And since the president made many of his decisions on the basis of information they supplied, the Domestic Council became one of the most important elements in the Nixon White House.

THE NEEDS OF THE VOTERS

Democratic theory generally asserts that government should respond, somehow, to the wishes of the voters. In order to see how this might work in practice two things are needed: first, an understanding of the directions the voters are capable of giving, and, second, some knowledge of how the government apprehends these cues and responds to them. This leads to something infrequently discussed, but vital to an understanding of how American democracy functions — the idea of the presidency as a representative institution.

A good deal is known about the level of voters' information about issues, and the relation of their issue views to their voting decision. This knowledge may be summarized in three propositions. First, the level of information for the average voter is not high. This does not mean that he doesn't have attitudes about the various policy areas, but simply that he does not have the detailed information to sustain a discussion about the nuances of policy. It is no more realistic to expect a voter to have a professional economist's command of fiscal policy in order to make judgments about prosperity than it is to demand the average person be a musicologist before he knows whether he likes Bach or rock. Second, there is a significant relationship between citizens' views about issues and the candidates they choose for president. In order to learn about this close association, one must first make realistic assumptions about what the voters do know, and then devise questions that allow them to respond to surveys in a way that reveals this knowledge. For example, if voters are permitted to locate their preferences along scales in the various policy areas (such as those used in this book), and if they further indicate where they perceive the candidates to be along the same policy scales, this information makes it possible to explain over half of the variance in the vote on the basis of issues alone. The voters' policy views are multidimensional, but along each of the dimensions they tend to vote for the candidate whose views are closest to their own.[7] Third, voters have more information about presidential candidates than senatorial or congressional candidates, and their views about policy are more closely related to their presidential votes than to their votes for senator or congressman. In 1968, 87 percent of the respondents in a nationwide survey were able to make two or more statements concerning what they liked or disliked about Richard Nixon or Hubert Humphrey. Only 52 percent of the respondents in states electing senators were able to make that number of statements about their senate candidates. Issue preferences were a little more likely to be associated with presidential than senatorial voting, and nonissue considerations such as party or simple name recognition were much more likely to be associated with senate voting than with presidential. And in 1972, 72 percent of the respondents in a Wisconsin study said they gave "a great deal" or "a moderate amount" of attention to the presidential campaign, whereas only 35 percent of them said they paid the same degree of attention to the congressional contests.[8] To recapitulate, voters' preferences about policy are quite general; there is a strong relationship between those preferences and presidential voting; the relationship between issue preference and voting does not exist with respect to the legislative branch. Thus, there is far better reason to say that the president receives an issue mandate from the voters than there is to make such a claim for the Congress.

If the voters are capable of giving intelligent, though broad, directions to the presidency, how capable is that institution of responding? More specifically, how well attuned was the Nixon administration to the wishes of the voters? We have seen that the voters were regarded as important. When asked about the views of various actors on the political stage, voters were seen by Domestic Council staff as second in importance only to the president himself. As Ward Norris put it:

> *Aside from the president himself, I try to give the utmost attention to the views of my colleagues, the voters, and the members of the cabinet. These are the people I'm responsive and responsible to.*

The data in Figure 3–1 (on page 53) show that the voters, cabinet members, and colleagues on the Domestic Council staff — in that order — were seen as somewhat more important than congressional leaders, and much more important than interest group spokesmen, bureau chiefs, and party leaders. So, the posture of the Domestic Council staff was to give heed to the voters' wishes.

Still more information about the relationship between voters' preferences and presidential policy may be found in Figure 5–1. Here data already presented are arrayed so that President Nixon's position in the policy areas (as perceived by his staff) may be compared directly with the preferences of Nixon and McGovern voters. In every case the Nixon position is located closer to that of the Nixon voters than to that of the McGovern voters. There are two policy areas — economic management and civil liberties — where there is a noticeable gap between the preferences of the president and those of the Nixon voters. Concretely, this means that Richard Nixon was more inclined to cut spending; opposed to price and wage controls, while voters were neutral; more opposed to using busing to achieve racial balance; and less willing to increase the authority of the police than were those who voted for him. The views of the president and the views of his voters, however, were quite similar in four of the six policy areas. With respect to international involvement, social benefits, natural resources, and agriculture, the Nixon voters put in office a man predisposed to execute almost exactly the policies they preferred. Further, if the president was the most important person and the voters were the next most influential group from the perspective of the Domestic Council staff, there is good reason to believe that these policy preferences would ultimately be reflected in the programs they drafted.

There is also a broader point implicit in Figure 5–1. Despite the heightened rhetoric of political campaigns, and the sometimes acrimonious disputes between rival officeholders, the actual debate over policy takes place within a rather confined range. There was debate over the use of price and wage controls in 1972, but no one was arguing for a totally regimented economy and no one was arguing for a "pure" free economy. No major candidate was calling for the elimination of the income tax, and very few voters thought there ought to be a drastic increase in federal spending. Similarly, it was difficult to find anyone who thought pollution should not be controlled. Specific examples could be multiplied, but a glance at

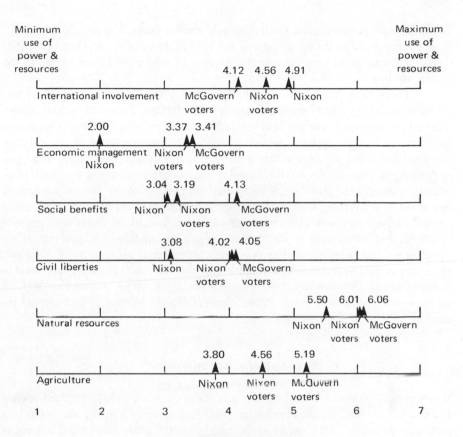

FIGURE 5–1

**Comparison of Staff Perceptions
of Nixon's Attitudes with Mean
Positions of Nixon and McGovern Voters**

Figure 5–1 does better. In every policy area[9] there was a consensus on the general direction of public policy. Debate takes place not on policy fundamentals but, rather, on the details. And the range within which this policy debate takes place is set by the candidates and the majority of the voters.

Now how did the Domestic Council relate to this policy consensus? The most important consideration here is where the weight of the president was put in this rather confined policy debate. On this point a statement by David Archer about instructions he had been given by the president is most illuminating:

> *His guidance was simply to get way in front of the conservatives, but stay behind those who would be so radical as not to consider the economic benefits and jobs in trying to clean up this problem.*

Given an issue debate confined to a relatively narrow range, and presidential directions to stay ahead of the conservatives and behind the radicals, one has conditions that should operate to keep the overall direction of public policy very close to the voters' desires.

There were many costs to the Watergate affair that dominated domestic political news for so many months after the 1972 election. Those revelations further reduced public trust in our political institutions at a time when there was an urgent need for precisely the opposite, and ultimately led to the resignation of the president himself. But when we review this evidence on the way the administration was responding to the wishes of the voters—the voters themselves casting issue-oriented votes for the president, a staff believing that the voters' wishes were more important than anything save the preferences of the president himself, a president elected whose own policy views were very close to those of the voters who put him in office, and instructions to his staff to stay in the middle of a genuine policy consensus—and the irony of the Watergate affair becomes even more apparent. Here was an administration whose relationship with the voters could be supported in terms of almost any democratic theory; yet because of actions contrary to the faith of democracy, its power to act dwindled away within months of a triumphal re-election.

THE NEEDS OF THE PRESIDENCY

Whether the Domestic Council staff, or any staff, meets the needs of the presidency is a much more difficult question to deal with than whether it fulfills the needs of a particular president or the needs of the voters. In the latter cases the evidence is rather straightforward. One need only show that the staff is working in a way that is congruent with the style of operation with which the president is most comfortable, or that it is aware of and responsive to the broad policy preferences of the electorate. The needs of the presidency, at least in terms of the analysis presented in the first chapter, present a more complex set of questions. Working within the constraints set by the political calendar, the staff must be able to operate effectively in a complex political environment in order to translate the preferences of the president and the voters into programs in half a dozen policy areas. There are many ways of doing this, depending on the work habits of the president, the attitudes and skills of the staff members, and the power situation in which they find themselves.

In the case of the Nixon presidency, the problem was how to produce programs reflecting an activist posture in international affairs and natural resources, moderate preferences in social benefits, civil liberties, and agriculture, and a conservative position on economic management, and to do this in an unfavorable power situation. The possibility of accomplishment was certainly not improved by so many of the power bases outside the White House being in unsympathetic hands. This condition set real limits on what the administration could hope to do. Yet an even more important question is how the president and his senior aides reacted to this adverse power situation.

The revelations coming out of the Watergate affair have shown a willingness to believe that others in Washington did not dissent in degree and detail, but that they were actively hostile to fundamental purposes of the administration. Max Ways, assessing Watergate as a management problem, concluded that "the distress was in their minds":

> *Powerful men in the White House came to think of themselves as inhabitants of a beleaguered and distressed city, surrounded by enemies whose strength and malice they exaggerated. An intense desire to win, coupled with the belief that the situation is desperate, can release a lot of energizing adrenalin. If it goes too far, such a state of mind can also trigger reckless misjudgments.* [10]

Elliot Richardson, who served the Nixon administration in four major posts, expressed a similar view when asked "What caused Watergate?":

> *It comes down to a whole set of attitudes toward the presidential and political process. . . . This has been a limitation of the Nixon presidency . . . the tragic flaw of his presidency.* [11]

Since some persons within the administration viewed political rivals as "enemies," he concluded, it became easy to use tactics that would be appropriate to use against genuine enemies.

Other attitudes about an adverse power situation are quite possible. Members of the Domestic Council staff recognized that many aspects of the political environment did not facilitate their tasks. They pointed to a lack of response from the bureaucracy, an unwillingness on the part of Congress to treat administration programs seriously, and a need for greater support from the general public. But there was little to suggest they saw themselves surrounded by "enemies." Statements that civil servants had narrow perspectives brought only reluctant assent. The political environment was seen as something to be mastered, at the very least something the staff members had to know well enough in order to interpret the cues and fragments of information they picked up from various sources. There was awareness of the need for good rapport with others, and of the effort necessary to achieve it. Frank Miller, for example, had said, "I think in fairness there is a constant battle to avoid agency paranoia and White House paranoia, and an intelligent approach with reasonably bright people can overcome a good deal of that."

How could such different attitudes exist in the same White House? Here it is well to remember how differentiated the White House has become; each specialized group develops attitudes and a behavior pattern of its own. Since I did not interview those on the political staffs who apparently did view rivals as "enemies," I do not know why they felt this way. I can offer some explanation about why such attitudes were less characteristic of the Domestic Council staff. One reason is that they were too busy with policy responsibilities to develop fantasies about the presumed motives of other politicians. Even more important, the nature of their tasks drew them into the environment. They had daily contact with agencies, congressmen, and interest group spokesmen, and that tended to inhibit the development of intergroup conflict. If communications between groups are reduced, there is a greater likelihood that they will develop divergent norms; if the norms are dissimilar, there is a tendency to interpret the behavior of other groups as hostile; if the activity of other groups is seen as inimical, communication between the groups is likely to be reduced. This is a well-known pattern of intergroup hostility.[12] Communication between groups is no guarantee that their relationships will become friendly, but lack of contact vastly increases the chances of antagonism.

How groups on the White House staff react to an adverse power situation is not only a critical question, but it is likely to be a continuing one. Of the 30 years between 1946 and 1976, 16 have been marked by Congresses organized by a party that did not elect a president, and unless and until some basic shifts in the partisan loyalties of the voters occur, the chances are good that any Republican president will face a Democratic Congress. Furthermore, Washington is full of the rivalries that could develop into outright hostility. Evidence of this can be seen in congressional complaints about their inability to break through the circle of presidential advisors, in White House comments about the archaic methods of decision-making on Capitol Hill, in the scornful way elected executives refer to bureaucrats, in the feeling of agency heads that politicians are too ready to shift their positions in response to transitory moods of the public, and so on. The low-level intergroup rivalry that these comments reflect is a key to understanding politics in Washington. Usually it is kept within tolerable bounds, so that each political group is able to relate to its environment without interpreting that environment as overly hostile. But the possibility of a president being held in check by an adverse power balance in a city already characterized by open rivalry is a volatile combination. Appointment of staff members who will concern themselves with program accomplishment rather than presumed threats to the president's power, and keeping the staff sufficiently small so that all staff members will have continuing and healthy contact with non-White House types may be necessary for a positive relationship between a White House group and its political environment. These conditions seem to have been met with the Domestic Council staff, but apparently not with some other elements of the Nixon White House retinue.

Regardless of the favorability or unfavorability of the power situation, the staff must be able to work within the constraints of a fixed political calendar and operate effectively in a complex environment in order to translate the preferences of the voters and the president into programs in the half-dozen policy areas. It follows from the limits of time granted them that some things are going to remain undone, and that the choices of those projects to which presidential energy shall be devoted are crucial to the success or failure of an administration. The consequent importance of presidential choice is reflected in the allocation of time of the Domestic Council staff, particularly in the three responsibilities to which most of their time was devoted. If presidential attention was to be devoted to top-priority goals, someone had to take care of the emergencies that otherwise would have been distracting. Hence, fire-engine chores inevitably occupied their time. As they gained experience, they came to realize that if they referred every question to the chief executive, the channels would become so clogged that nothing would get done. Hence, they (or at least the leaders) began to make a number of decisions themselves. As they learned more about the complexity of politics, they began to appreciate just how many implications were contained in each presidential choice. Hence, clarification of options was given their utmost attention.

It is not surprising that several analyses point to choice — and the conditions that facilitate choice — as central elements in the presidency. Richard Neustadt believes that staff can help a president do his job, but he does not think that staff can substitute for what the president fails to comprehend himself.

> *A president is helped by what gets into his mind. His first essential need is information. . . . (But) it is not information of a general sort that helps a president see (his) personal stakes; not summaries, not surveys, not the bland amalgams. Rather . . . it is the odds and ends of tangible detail that pieced together in his mind illuminate the underside of issues put before him. To help himself he must reach out as widely as he can for every scrap of fact, opinion, gossip, bearing on his interests and relationships as president.* [13]

Alexander George argues that the kinds of problems confronting the president are characterized by patterns of multiple causation, and the critical aspects of the decisions he makes are most likely to be revealed by a system of multiple advocacy. Professor George thinks this so important that he would relieve the special assistant (for national security affairs, in the case he is discussing) from all other responsibilities, such as being a policy advocate, or an implementer of decisions once they are taken. Instead, the special assistant should be the custodian of the process.

> *. . . The task central to the custodian's role . . . is to find ways of maintaining and improving the workings of the policy-making system. This the custodian attempts to do on behalf of the executive by balancing actor resources when necessary, by strengthening weaker advocates, or compensating for their weakness, by bringing in new advisers to argue for unpopular options, by setting new channels of information so that the president and the other policy makers are not dependent on a single channel of information, by arranging for independent evaluation of decisional premises that are not*

receiving competent, objective evaluation within the system, by monitoring the policy-making process for possibly dangerous malfunctions and instituting appropriate corrective action. [14]

Keith Clark and Laurence Legere point to decision-making as one of a series of closely related areas in which the president needs help. "The President needs to have some way of exploring alternatives and evaluating consequences. He needs to understand not only the substantive background of the issues, but also their bureaucratic and political implications," [15] Over and over the words reoccur: Get all the information that bears on a decision, turn up enough so the president will have every scrap and every clue that might give him the insight he needs to make a wise decision. This is nearly what the Domestic Council staff members said themselves when asked about institutional imperatives. Tom Parsons said what must be done was:

To make sure that we have done the best job possible of determining the facts and alternative solutions when the president has to make a decision.

And Mark Jensen commented:

The must part of it is that we must explore all possible, even the dead end, routes, and tell him why they're dead end, at least cover the waterfront in the case of disgorging information . . . Our job is to make sure that there is not simply a single point of view being presented so that the president does know even if he's made a wrong choice, that at least it's with conscious knowledge of what the consequences will be. And nobody's so omniscient as to be able to determine all the possibilities, but our function is to be as exhaustive as we can be.

This is a case where academic observers and actual participants are close to agreement. What institutional analysts had posited as a central need of the presidency was the goal staff members had set for themselves. Neither academics nor activists were under any illusion that staff or president would be able to avoid mistakes. Professors Neustadt and George were quite aware they were presenting ideal models; Mark Jensen was frank to admit that no one was so omniscient as to be able to determine all the possibilities. No real-life presidency can do more than approximate an ideal presidency. But as long as the staff gives detailed consideration to the range of politically viable options, and as long as the president ponders those choices in full awareness of the multiple purposes for which the enormous powers of the office have been granted, the presidency will be well served.

SUMMARY

There are three questions to be asked in assessing any White House staff. How well did it serve the personal needs of the president? The Domestic Council staff prepared detailed written analyses for the private contemplation Richard Nixon preferred. How well did it serve the needs of the voters? The Domestic Council staff was generally aware of and responsive to the policy preferences of the voters. How well did it serve the needs of the presidency? That is a more complex question because of the multiple sources of administration behavior, but the Domestic Council staff was able to relate to an adverse power situation without becoming embittered, and they did focus their attention on facilitating the essential task of presidential decision-making.

NOTES

[1]Theodore H. White, *The Making of the President —1968* (New York: Atheneum, 1969), p. 145.

[2]Theodore H. White, *The Making of the President —1972* (New York: Atheneum, 1973), p. 351.

[3]Frank Cormier, "Nixon's Decision Process: He's Not an Agonizer," *Washington Star-News*, November 13, 1972, p. D-20.

[4]Rufus P. Browning, "The Interaction between Personality and Political System in Decisions to Run for Office," *Journal of Social Issues*, July, 1968, pp. 93–109.

[5]White, *Making of the President —1972*, p. 355.

[6]Ted Knap, "FAA chief deals blow to Nixon," *Columbus Citizen-Journal*, July 25, 1974, p. 10.

[7]Comparative State Election Project, *Explaining the Vote: Presidential Choices in the Nation and the States, 1968* (Chapel Hill, North Carolina: Institute for Research in Social Science, 1974).

[8]Barbara Hinckley, C. Richard Hofstetter, and John Kessel, "Information and the Vote: A Comparative Election Study," *American Politics Quarterly*, April, 1974, pp. 131–158; Barbara Hinckley, "Issues, Information Costs, and Congressional Elections" (mimeo, 1973).

[9]There was one exception, which ought to be noted. The consensus figures on the individual items in Table 3–2 on page 57 show a lack of agreement on the use of economic controls. There was, however, a strong consensus on cutting government spending, the other item in this policy area.

[10]Max Ways, "Watergate as a Case Study in Management," *Fortune*, November, 1973, p. 196.

[11]Guy Halverson, "Richardson views Nixon," *Christian Science Monitor*, January 24, 1974, p. 4.

[12]Theodore M. Newcomb, Ralph H. Turner, and Philip E. Converse, *Social Psychology* (New York: Holt, Rinehart & Winston, 1965), p. 447.

[13]Richard E. Neustadt, *Presidential Power* (New York: Wiley, 1960), pp. 153–154. See also the fine explication of Neustadt's analysis: Peter W. Sperlich, "Bargaining and Overload: An Essay on Presidential Power," in Aaron Wildavsky, ed., *The Presidency* (Boston: Little, Brown, 1969), pp. 168–192.

[14]Alexander George, "The Case for Multiple Advocacy in Making Foreign Policy," *American Political Science Review*, September, 1972, p. 783.

[15]Keith C. Clark and Laurence J. Legere, eds., *The President and the Management of National Security* (New York: Praeger, 1969), pp. 56–57.

Appendix A

Indexes and Measures

A2.1 RESPONDENT'S ATTITUDES ABOUT POLICY

Attitudes about policy were measured along a seven-point scale by means of a card-sort of the type devised by Lester Milbrath and his colleagues. The respondent is given a series of cards containing brief statements, such as "Government spending should be cut" or "Farmers should be guaranteed a good income." He is asked to indicate his own attitude about each statement by placing the card containing the statement in one of seven locations along a sort board, as shown in Figure A–1. Each square on the sort board is marked to correspond to the respondent's own reaction to the stimulus statement: strongly disagree $(--)$, disagree $(-)$, slightly disagree $(-)$, not sure (0), slightly agree $(+)$, agree $(++)$, strongly agree $(+++)$. Therefore, each statement can be given a score from 1 to 7 (or -3 to $+3$, if

FIGURE A–1

A Sort Board

one prefers) indicating the extent of the person's agreement or disagreement with the item.

In measuring attitudes about the policy areas, two stimulus statements were used for international involvement, economic management, social welfare, and civil liberties. The attitude score reported in Chapter 2 is based on the mean of the two scores for each policy area. Single statements were used for natural resources and agriculture, and these scores are reported directly. (See Appendix B for a complete list of the items.) In each case a high score was employed if the reaction favored use of government authority and/or resources, while a low score denoted the opposite reaction. (If the statement was worded so that agreement would not call for government action and/or spending, as "Government spending should be cut," the scores were reversed for that item.) Thus an attitude score of 7 corresponds to "maximum use of power and resources" and a score of 1 corresponds to "minimum use of power and resources."

Measuring staff attitudes in this way was inadequate in two respects. The staff members' information level was too high for these terse statements to capture the wealth of policy detail within their ken. For example, in considering the assertion "Welfare payments should be increased," one person commented: "There are fifteen hundred welfare programs. Some of them should be increased; some of them should be decreased; some of them should be abolished." In addition, with only one or two statements within each policy area, there are serious difficulties with measurement reliability. On a seven-point scale, if a person's "true" response is "slightly disagree," the least possible measurement error ($\pm$ 1) runs from "disagree" to "not sure," almost half of the scale. When there are enough items, one can assume that high and low errors cancel out, thus allowing the measured response to converge with the "true" response. There were not enough items within policy areas to make this assumption.

There were also some substantial advantages to this form of attitude measurement. Since the respondent reads each items himself, this portion of the interview proceeds at "eye-speed" rather than the slower "vocal-speed" necessary when the interviewer reads material aloud. Hence, more information can be picked up. This was particularly important in interviewing White House aides whose time was quite limited. Use of a seven magnitude scale rests on findings of George Miller and Charles Osgood that this yields optimum natural discrimination. (Use of a five magnitude scale does not ask most respondents to discriminate so much as they are able; use of a nine magnitude scale forces artificial choices to correspond to response categories.) The individual stimulus items were carefully selected to reflect dimensions of debate within each policy area. And these items, while terse, did refer to the types of questions policy-makers must decide. The policy-maker does not have to make up his mind whether he supports some abstract liberal or conservative doctrine. A more typical decision concerns what kind of government regulation or how great an expenditure for what purpose will be most effective in dealing with the delivery of health care, the property tax, the prevention of pollution, or some other concrete problem. Questions dealing with specific policy areas are more likely to tap attitudes actually related to these decisions.

A2.2 STANDARD DEVIATION

The standard deviation is the most commonly used measure of variability about a mean. Its properties are such that if the distribution is normal, roughly two-thirds of the cases may be expected to fall within $\pm$ one standard deviation, and 19 cases out of 20 may be expected to occur within just under $\pm$ two standard deviations. The computational formula is:

$$\sigma = 1/N \ \sqrt{N\Sigma X^2 - (\Sigma X)^2}$$

Used as a measure of agreement among members of a population, a low standard deviation would indicate that a consensus exists, and a high standard deviation would indicate a lack of consensus.

In this instance, the N for the Domestic Council staff members is 16. With so few cases it would be inappropriate to rely on the standard deviation as a descriptive statistic. For the general public, however, the mean N for these items is 704. Therefore the staff standard deviation can be interpreted by means of comparison with the standard deviation for the general public, since the latter N is clearly large enough to permit calculation of the statistic.

A2.3 CONSENSUS

The direct measure of consensus is based on the assumption that if a consensus does exist, responses should fall into the mode, and the fact that the minimum measurement error is $\pm$ one magnitude. Therefore one is justified in comparing the number of responses actually falling into the mode and two adjacent categories and the number that would be expected to do so if there was an equal distribution of answers in each category on the scale. This leads to the formula:

$$\text{Consensus} = \left(\frac{\text{frequency observed} - \text{frequency expected}}{N - \text{frequency expected}} \right)$$

The consensus measure takes on values bounded by $+1.0$ and

$$\left(\frac{n - f_e}{N - f_e} \right)$$

where n is the minimum number of responses that could occur in the modal category. A value of $+1.0$ occurs when there is complete consensus, that is, when all responses fall into the mode and the two adjacent categories. A value of 0 occurs when there is no more agreement than would be expected by chance, that is, when the number of cases in the mode and two adjacent categories is just that expected if the responses were equally distributed among all categories. Negative values occur when there is disagreement. This would imply that the largest number of responses are not falling into adjacent magnitudes; in other words, when one subgroup agrees with a statement, and another disagrees.

Given seven magnitudes and 16 respondents, an equal distribution of responses would imply that no more than seven responses should occur in three adjacent magnitudes. Hence the consensus measure is $(f_o - 7)/9$ for this case. Any value greater than .22 indicates that a majority of the staff attitudes fall into the mode and two adjacent categories.

A2.4 PROXIMITY

The measure of proximity depends on determining how much attitudinal distance exists. We want the proximity measure to take on a high value when attitudes of the objects being compared (e.g., two persons, a person and a group, two groups, etc.) are similar, and we want the measure to take on a low value when the attitudes are dissimilar. Therefore the formula is:

$$\text{Proximity} = \left(\frac{\text{maximum att. distance} - \text{observed att. distance}}{\text{maximum attitudinal distance}} \right)$$

This means that the proximity measure will equal 1.0 if the attitudes are identical, and 0 if the attitudes are at the opposite ends of whatever scale is being used.

Since we have separate scores in six different policy areas, they are first written in vector form. The elements of the vector are ordered: (international involvement, economic management, social welfare, civil liberties, natural resources, agriculture). Thus a vector of (6,2,3,2,5,1) would denote a score of 6 in international involvement, a score of 2 in economic management, a score of 3 in social welfare, and so forth. Now let us assume a second vector, (4,3,3,4,5,4). The attitudinal distance between these two vectors would be determined by taking the absolute difference between each corresponding pair of elements:

$$
\begin{array}{c}
(6,\ 2,\ 3,\ 2,\ 5,\ 1) \\
(4,\ 3,\ 3,\ 4,\ 5,\ 4) \\
\hline
(2,\ 1,\ 0,\ 2,\ 0,\ 3)
\end{array}
$$

The elements in the resulting vector, (2,1,0,2,0,3), represent the attitudinal distance along each of the six dimensions.

This vector may be reduced to a scalar measure by taking the sum of the elements. To do that, one has to be willing to sacrifice the dimensionality of the vector in exchange for the convenience of a summary measure. One must further assume that the dimensions are of equal importance. (Otherwise, one would have to weight the elements according to his judgment of their relative importance, and then divide the resulting summation by the sum of the weights.) With those assumptions, the vector in our example may be reduced, thus:

$$(2 + 1 + 0 + 2 + 0 + 3) = 8$$

Therefore we conclude the attitudinal distance represented by the two vectors with which we began has a value of 8.

Since the maximum value that can be attained by our measure of attitudinal distance is 36 (that is, a distance of 6 along each of 6 dimensions), the proximity measure in this example would be:

$$\begin{aligned} \text{Proximity} &= (36 - 8)/36 \\ &= 28/36 \\ &= .78 \end{aligned}$$

A2.5 COMMUNICATION

The existence of communication links was established by asking "Which persons do you spend the most time with in getting your own work done?" and then assuming that if a respondent said he was spending time with another person, he was probably sending messages to him. This question has a high reliability. A test-retest correlation of .9 has been obtained with it in studying executives. (See Ralph M. Stogdill, "Interlocking Methods of Organizational Study," in Robert K. Merton *et al.*, eds., *Reader in Bureaucracy* [Glencoe, Ill.: The Free Press, 1952], p. 445.)

A2.6 INFLUENCE

Separate means were used to identify each of the four ways in which influence might be exercised. It was simply assumed that each person recognized the legitimacy of his institutional superiors. Hence each staff leader was credited with exercising legitimate influence over those working under his direction. In the cases of identification, expertise, and sanctions, questions were adapted from the Bay Area study. The question dealing with identification was, "Among members of the Council staff, who would you say is the *most respected*? I mean the kind of man a new member would look up to when he's just learning about the Council and how it works." On expertise, the item read, "Are there any staff members who are especially *expert* in their areas of Council work? Individuals who are always fully informed and particularly influential for that reason?" The question alluding to sanctions was, "If there is disagreement among staff members, which member's opposition would you be most concerned about?'' (For the wording of the corresponding questions from the Bay Area study, see Eulau and Prewitt, *Labyrinths of Democracy,* pp. 662, 661, 654.) Other staff members mentioned by each person in response to these questions were considered to have the potential of exercising that kind of influence over the respondent. For example, when another staff member's name was given in answer to the question about who was most respected, I took this to mean that the respondent himself respected the man whose name had been mentioned. Thus when Archer said that Gruber and Leggett were respected, entries were made in the cells in Archer's row of the influence matrix in Gruber's and Leggett's columns to denote one-stage influence (by means of respect) over Archer.

A3.1 RELATIVE IMPORTANCE OF OTHER ACTORS

The assessment of the relative importance of other persons was based on responses to a single question: "Now this is a little more difficult, because it refers to a hypothetical situation. I'm going to name some persons and groups. In each case I'd like you to *assume* that you'd found out they had *very strong* views about some topic you were handling. How much difference would this make in the way *you* handled it—a *very great* difference, a *great* difference, *some* difference, *hardly any* difference, or *no* difference at all?''
> *a. Colleagues on the Domestic Council Staff*
> *b. Interest Group Spokesmen*
> *c. The President*
> *d. Voters*
> *e. Congressional Leaders*
> *f. Republican Party Leaders*
> *g. Cabinet Members*
> *h. Bureau Chiefs*

This was an instance in which a question yielded information of a different character from what I had had in mind when I wrote it. I put it in the questionnaire simply as a validity check on the card-sort. Included in the card-sort were items asking for the respondent's perception of the views of the president and the views of the voters. I was assuming that the staff member's own attitudes and his perceptions of the attitudes of the president and of the voters would be the three most important influences on his own behavior. Still, I wanted to check on the possibility that others might be more important than either the president or the voters, and I included the question for that reason.

The question did serve as a validity check (the president and the voters had the two highest scores), but it did much more that I had not anticipated. The respondents all found the query difficult to answer, and virtually all asked for a clarification. I replied by trying to restate the question so as not to lead them in one direction or another. This conversation usually continued until they had given answers to the first two or three actors listed. At that point the respondents became a little more comfortable and were able to proceed with fewer questions about my intent. They continued, however, to embellish their answers by telling me about their relationships with "congressional leaders" or "bureau chiefs" or whomever. The result of all this conversation was to provide a great deal of information about the staff members' relationship to others in their environment. It would have been hard to write a question that would have elicited the information directly because I didn't know enough (before the interviews when the questionnaire was constructed) to know what to ask. Hence, this was an example of a bad question that brought forth some useful information.

The importance scores reported in Figure 3–1 were calculated by giving a value of 1 to an answer that the actor's views would make a very great difference, 2 to great difference, 3 to some difference, 4 to hardly any difference, and 5 to no difference at all. The mean scores are based on 15 responses for president, staff colleagues, and interest group spokesmen, and 14 responses for the other actors.

A3.2 STAFF PERCEPTIONS OF PRESIDENT NIXON'S ATTITUDES

These perceptions were ascertained by means of a card-sort. In each case where the respondent's own attitude was determined by his reaction to a statement such as "Government spending should be cut" or "Farmers should be guaranteed a good income," parallel statements read "President Nixon favors cutting government spending" and "President Nixon believes farmers should be guaranteed a good income." Staff responses to the perceptual items were scored in the same way as their responses to the items concerning their own attitudes.

The details of the scoring procedure are given in A2.1 above, and the full list of items concerning their perceptions of President Nixon's attitudes is given in Appendix B.

A3.3 CONSENSUS ABOUT NIXON'S ATTITUDES

All of the consensus measures in Table 3–1 are based on the formula:

$$\text{Consensus} = \left(\frac{\text{frequency observed} - \text{frequency expected}}{N - \text{frequency expected}} \right)$$

which is discussed in A2.3 above.

The figures on consensus among staff members reflect the consensus resulting from their own attitudes. These figures for the individual items have already been reported in Table 2–1. Where there are two items in a policy area, the consensus figure for the policy area is the mean; where only one item referred to a policy area, the figures are the same.

The figures for consensus on perception of the president are calculated in the same manner. The only difference is that the raw data come from the responses concerning President Nixon's attitudes.

The values of the consensus measure on perception of the president by specialists are also based on the same formula. Here the input data are restricted to perceptions of President Nixon's attitudes on the part of those staff members who reported spending a great deal of time or a fair amount of time dealing with the policy area in question. (See A4.2 below for a discussion of this.) The values of the consensus measure among specialists vary more widely because of the low number of respondents in some policy areas. Some 12 staff members said they were spending at least a fair amount of time on economic management, and 13 did so in social welfare, but the Ns in civil liberties, natural resources, and agriculture were 8, 5, and 4, respectively.

A3.4 ATTITUDES OF THE GENERAL PUBLIC

Identically worded card-sort items were included in a survey of the general public conducted during the 1972 election campaign. Both Domestic Council staff members and voters indicated their own attitudes on economic management, for example, by the way they responded to "Wages and prices should be controlled by the government" and "Government spending should be cut."

A3.5 STAFF PERCEPTIONS OF PUBLIC ATTITUDES

As was the case with staff perceptions of President Nixon's attitudes, parallel items asked about the staff perceptions of the attitudes of voters. In the case of economic management, the stimulus items read "American voters believe wages and prices should be controlled by the government" and "American voters favor cutting government spending."

A3.6 CONSENSUS AMONG THE GENERAL PUBLIC

The measure of consensus among the general public was based on the formula

$$\text{Consensus} = \left(\frac{\text{frequency observed} - \text{frequency expected}}{N - \text{frequency expected}}\right)$$

discussed in A2.3 above. The data were drawn from a national survey conducted just before the 1972 election.

The average number of respondents for these items on public policy was 704. With an *N* of this size, one could expect almost exactly 3/7 of the responses to fall into three adjacent categories if they are evenly distributed. If the measure has a value of greater than .13, this means the consensus contains more than a majority.

This measure assumes that there will be a unimodal distribution if a consensus exists. Perhaps the best way to understand the consequences of this unimodal assumption is to look at two distributions. The first, "The government should act to stop pollution," produced a unimodal distribution; the second, "The government ought to help pay everyone's medical bills," produced a bimodal distribution. The distributions were:

	− − −	− −	−	0	+	+ +	+ + +
Pollution	1.8%	1.8%	1.5%	5.7%	9.5%	41.2%	38.5%
Medical Bills	14.8%	25.9%	10.8%	8.8%	13.5%	15.1%	11.2%

In the case of controlling pollution, 41.2 percent of all responses fell into the mode, and an additional 45.3 percent fell into the two adjacent categories. Since this is well in excess of the 42.9 percent that would be expected if the responses were distributed evenly, the consensus measure takes on a very high value of .81. In the bimodal case concerning medical bills, 51.5 percent of the responses fall into the mode and two adjacent categories. Some 39.8 percent of the responses, however, indicate some degree of agreement with government aid in payment of medical bills, and 8.8 percent are not sure. The consensus measure is sensitive to this, and the low value of .15 denotes that barely more than a majority fall into the range of consensus. It should also be noted that when there is a unimodal distribution the mean and the mode have similar values; whereas with a bimodal distribution, the mean tends toward the center of the scale. In the unimodal pollution example, the mode was 6 (++) and the mean was 5.97. In the bimodal medical costs example, the mode was 2(−−), but the mean was 3.70. Therefore a choice to base one's measure on the mean or the mode can lead to different conclusions, if the opinions are distributed in other than a unimodal fashion.

A word also ought to be said about the representativeness of the preliminary data set that was used for this analysis. The average number of responses to these items was 704. The lowest number of respondents was 683; the highest was 725. These numbers are rather low for a national sample. Moreover, this data set contained only 789 cases out of 1,039 in the full data set. However, the study design was constructed as a quasi-panel in four waves. Each quarter of the interviews was to be representative in and of itself. The data set available for analysis contained roughly the first three waves of interviews. Therefore one can be more confident of the representativeness of the data than would normally be the case with an *N* of this size.

A3.7 STAFF PERCEPTION OF PUBLIC CONSENSUS

Again, the same basic formula for consensus is used, but the data employed are those appropriate to determine the extent to which the staff perceives a public consensus. The data used are those discussed in A3.3 and A3.4 above: the basic items administered to the general public, and the parallel items about the positions favored by voters administered to the staff. The modal category is the category chosen by the largest number of staff members as the preference of the voters. The distribution of responses (in that category and the two immediately adjacent to determine the observed frequency) is taken from the responses of the general public.

The implication of this measure is that perceptual accuracy on the part of the staff depended on two things: first, the existence of a consensus on the part of the general public, and, second, the ability of the staff to understand where the most voters were located. If the modal category of the staff members coincides with the mode for the general public, the value of the consensus measure will be the same as it is for the general public. If the modal perception of the staff members does not coincide with the actual mode of the general public, the value of the measure will be lower. How much lower depends on what proportion of the public responses fall into the mode selected by the staff and the two adjacent categories. In no case can the measure take on a value higher than that for the general public.

A3.8 CORRELATIONS BETWEEN STAFF ATTITUDES, PUBLIC ATTITUDES, AND STAFF PERCEPTIONS OF PUBLIC ATTITUDES

The correlations between these attitudes and perceptions can be best visualized by thinking of a triangular relationship among the public attitudes, the staff attitudes, and the staff perceptions of the public attitudes. The correlations shown in Figure A–2 are Pearson product-moment correlations, for which the computational formula is:

$$ r = \frac{N\Sigma XY - (\Sigma X)(\Sigma Y)}{\sqrt{[N\Sigma X^2 - (\Sigma X)^2][N\Sigma Y^2 - (\Sigma Y)^2]}} $$

These figures represent the extent to which there is a linear relationship between any two of the variables. Thus the values in Figure A–2 suggest there is the strongest linear relationship between the policy preferences of the staff members and the policy preferences of the general public. When these coefficients of correlation are squared, they are called coefficients of determination, and they represent one's ability to predict one variable on the basis of information about another. Specifically, the value tells how much improvement would take place in your ability to predict, say, the public attitudes by knowing what the staff perceptions were over your prediction if you lacked any information about the staff perceptions. These values (often called r^2) are .53 between staff attitudes and public attitudes, .31

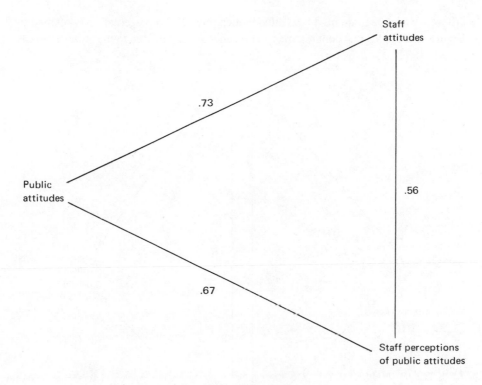

FIGURE A–2

between staff attitudes and staff perceptions of public attitudes, and .45 between public attitudes and staff perceptions. When we control the correlation between the public attitudes and the staff perceptions for the fact that both of these are related to the staff members' own attitudes (which is called calculating a first-order partial correlation), the correlation coefficient (r) becomes .47, and the r^2 becomes .22. A comparison of the coefficients of determination when the effects of staff attitudes are controlled (.22) and when they are not controlled (.45) tells us that roughly half of our ability to predict public attitudes on the basis of staff perceptions is due to the staff members' own attitudes.

It is important to remember that these correlation figures do *not* tell us anything about identity of attitudes or whether or not any bias is being introduced. That is too often forgotten in enthusiastic attempts to read too much into statistical analysis. In fact, if you compare the correlation values in Figure A–2 with the information in Table 3–3, you will find that in this case the correlation is higher when bias is being introduced than when it is not.

Since this analysis resembles a well-known analysis of representation by Warren E. Miller and Donald E. Stokes, it would be well to point out some differences between them. The Miller-Stokes model of representation, sketched in Figure A–3, holds that congressmen's roll call votes are related to the attitudes of the

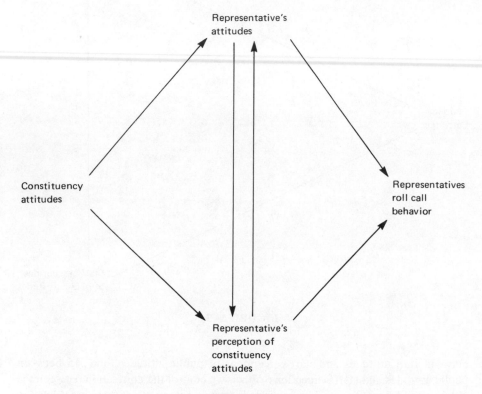

FIGURE A–3

constituencies they represent by paths that lead through the representatives' own attitudes and the representatives' perceptions of the constituency attitudes. The present analysis, while inspired by the earlier work of Miller and Stokes, varies in three ways. First, only the "left half" of the model is replicated. There was no simple measurable dependent variable to correspond to the congressmen's roll call votes. Second, I could do much less in the way of analysis. This study focused on the Domestic Council staff as a group. Individual-level data necessary for a more detailed investigation of perceptual accuracy were not collected. Third, the correlations reported by Miller and Stokes from their 1958 study were correlations across constituencies. The correlations reported here are correlations across policy areas.

A3.9 GENERAL ATTITUDES OF STAFF MEMBERS

There were several card-sort items that asked for the respondent's views about government structure or actors involved in the governmental process. The wording of these is given both in Table 3–4 and in Appendix B, and the score for each must be interpreted in the light of the wording of the statement itself. There was no common dimension to these statements. In every case a low score denotes disagreement with the item, and a high score denotes agreement. Specifically, 1 = strongly disagree, 2 = disagree, 3 = slightly disagree, 4 = not sure, 5 = slightly agree, 6 = agree, and 7 = strongly agree.

A4.1 TIME USE BY ACTIVITY

Data on this were gathered by handing each respondent a card on which five assignments were listed:

1. Backstopping the president by "fire-engine" chores when answers are needed in a hurry.

2. Collecting information and developing long-range forecasts on national needs.

3. Monitoring agency activity to be fully aware of the ways ongoing programs are being administered.

4. Clarifying options among issues being presented for decision.

5. Determining priorities to govern the use of presently available resources.

Each person was asked to state whether he spent "a great deal of time," "a fair amount of time," "not too much time," or "no time at all" on each of these activities. A score of 4 was assigned to "a great deal of time," 3 to "a fair amount of time," 2 to "not too much time," and 1 to "no time at all." Therefore a high score means that more time is being spent on a given assignment, and a low score means that less time is being spent on the assignment.

Each of the statements about types of activities was a paraphrase of one of the five policy functions listed by President Nixon in his March, 1970, message about the Domestic Council. This reflected a decision about research strategy. Some of the functions—for example, "identifying alternative ways of achieving these objectives, and recommending consistent, integrated sets of policy choices"—could have been separated into two distinct activities. I chose to stay with the five functions in order to provide a more direct answer to the question: Of the things the Domestic Council was originally intended to do, what is it actually doing?

A4.2 TIME USE BY ISSUE AREA

In this case, respondents were given a card in which issue areas were defined by specifying some issues that fell into each category:

1. International Involvement
(including foreign relations, national defense, Vietnam)
2. Economic Management
(including labor, jobs, taxation, fiscal or monetary policy, business regulation, transportation)
3. Social Welfare
(including health, welfare, community development, education, science, arts, humanities)
4. Civil Liberties
(including law enforcement, civil rights, life styles of individuals)
5. Natural Resources
(including energy production, air or water pollution, public lands, recreation, wildlife)
6. Agriculture
(including production of food or fiber, agricultural economics, rural development)

In each case the individual was asked to tell whether he spent "a great deal of time," "a fair amount of time," "not too much time," or "no time at all." As with the time analysis of assignments, high scores mean more time was spent on the issue area in question. Specifically, 4 = a great deal of time, 3 = a fair amount of time, 2 = not too much time, and 1 = no time at all.

Appendix B

Interview Schedule

I chose to conduct this research with a structured questionnaire. Much of the literature on elite interviewing counsels against this approach. The common argument is that when interviewing busy, important individuals, the interviewer should simply raise the topics he wants to discuss, and allow the respondents to tell what they regard as important. The counterargument is that while structured interviews do introduce some element of artificiality into the conversation, the opportunity to obtain standard information permits one to do so much more in the later analysis as to quite outweigh any problem resulting from using the structured questionnaire. That argument was certainly supported by my experience. Moreover, I found that the Domestic Council aides did not object to the form of the interview. One or two respondents asked about some of the individual questions, but that did not pose any problem to the interview. The average interview ran between forty-five minutes and an hour. The two shortest were just under half an hour; three interviews took half a morning. When respondents were not pressed for time they frequently embellished their answers, giving me details that were important to know about the Domestic Council but that I had not asked about. The result was that I gained the analytical power of the structured interview, and some of the rich detail one hopes for in a less focused conversation.

I tried to pare the interview schedule down to essential information in order to conserve time. In particular, I threw out a number of validity checks (i.e., questions that ask again about a topic in a slightly different way) after "test" interviews with two Council staff members had run over an hour. I decided to rely on single questions about a variety of subjects. There were multiple questions about what the respondents were doing with their time (Questions 4, 5, and 7), and some of the questions about relations with agencies (Questions 15, 16, and 17) yielded parallel information. Otherwise, additional questions on almost every topic would have been useful. To the thoughtful reader's query, wouldn't it have been useful to have had more information about . . . (almost every topic I discuss), the answer is an unequivocal "yes." The problem is that additional information about any one topic would have been purchased at the price of no information about something else I thought important.

The interview schedule, as the research itself, was affected by group concepts from Heinz Eulau and Kenneth Prewitt's *Labyrinths of Democracy,* the insights of Thomas E. Cronin's *The State of the Presidency,* and the policy areas developed in Aage Clausen's *How Congressmen Decide.* Questions borrowed or adapted from the Bay Area study are marked *, and a † denotes items suggested by Cronin's analysis of White House government. All the card-sort items concerning the policy areas were discussed with my colleagues Aage Clausen and C. Richard Hofstetter.

The interview schedule I used was:

I'd like to begin with some very general questions.

*1. Overall, just what makes the Domestic Council tick? I mean, *besides* the formal responsibilities, the flow of paper work, and such, who decides what the Council should do, and how does it work?

2. What would you say are the things the Council *must* do in order to serve the needs of the president?

3. And in your opinion what are the most important problems now confronting the administration?

Now I'd like to turn to your personal responsibilities.

4. In a general way, how would you describe your own job?

4a. (Assistant directors only.) Who are the members of your staff?

5. Next I'd like you to pick some specific project you're handling, one that is typical of the work you're doing, and that you're free to talk about. Could you tell me a little about this?

6. In view of your own responsibilities, how much time do you devote to each of the issue areas listed on this card? (Hand respondent Card A.) Do you spend a *great deal* of time, a *fair amount* of time, *not too much* time, or *no time at all* on matters falling within each of these issue areas?

Card A

Time Analysis of Issue Areas

1. International involvement
(including foreign relations, national defense, Vietnam)

2. Economic management
(including labor, jobs, taxation, fiscal or monetary policy, business regulation, transportation)

3. Social welfare
(including health, welfare, community development, education, science, arts, humanities)

4. Civil liberties
(including law enforcement, civil rights, life styles of individuals)

5. Natural resources
(including energy production, air or water pollution, public lands, recreation, wildlife)

6. Agriculture
(including production of food or fiber, agricultural economics, rural development)

Time Options: Great deal —Fair amount —Not too much —No time at all

---

7. Another way of looking at your job is the kind of assignments you have. Do you spend a *great deal* of time, a *fair amount* of time, *not too much* time, or *no time at all* on each of the assignments listed on this card? [Hand Respondent Card B.]

Card B

Time Analysis of Assignments

1. Backstopping the president by "fire-engine" chores when answers are needed in a hurry

2. Collecting information and developing long-range forecasts on national needs

3. Monitoring agency activity to be fully aware of the ways ongoing programs are being administered

4. Clarifying options among issues being presented for decision

5. Determining priorities to govern the use of presently available resources

Time Options: Great Deal —Fair amount —Not too much —No time at all

---

8. Now this is a little more difficult, because it refers to a hypothetical situation. I'm going to name some persons and groups. In each case I'd like you to *assume* that you'd found out they had *very strong* views about some topic you were handling. How much difference would it make in the way *you* handled it—a *very great* difference, a *great* difference, *some* difference, *hardly any* difference, or *no* difference at all?

    a. Colleagues on the Domestic Council staff
    b. Interest group spokesmen
    c. The president
    d. Voters
    e. Congressional leaders
    f. Republican party leaders

     g. Cabinet members
     h. Bureau chiefs

    9. Card-Sort. In the card-sort each respondent was given a series of cards—arranged randomly, so that no respondent saw the cards in the same order—each containing a brief statement. The respondent was asked to indicate his opinion about the stimulus statement by placing the card in one of seven squares on a sort-board, a sketch of which appears in Figure A–1 on page 125. The squares were marked to correspond to seven possible degrees of disagreement or agreement: strongly disagree $(--)$, disagree $(-)$, slightly disagree $(-)$, not sure (0), slightly agree $(+)$, agree $(++)$, and strongly agree $(+++)$. The stimulus items were:
     a. The United States should help countries all over the world.
     b. President Nixon believes the United States should help countries all over the world.
     c. American voters favor helping countries all over the world.
     d. America should spend whatever necessary for a strong military force.
     e. President Nixon favors spending whatever necessary for a strong military force.
     f. American voters favor spending whatever necessary for a strong military force.
     g. Wages and prices should be controlled by the government.
     h. President Nixon believes wages and prices should be controlled by the government.
     i. American voters believe wages and prices should be controlled by the government.
     j. Government spending should be cut.
     k. President Nixon favors cutting government spending.
     l. American voters favor cutting government spending.
     m. The government ought to help pay everyone's medical bills.
     n. President Nixon believes the government should help pay everyone's medical bills.
     o. American voters favor having the government help pay everyone's medical bills.
     p. Welfare payments ought to be increased.
     q. President Nixon favors increasing welfare payments.
     r. American voters favor increasing welfare payments.
     s. Busing should not be used to achieve a racial balance in schools.
     t. President Nixon believes busing should not be used to achieve a racial balance in schools.
     u. American voters do not favor using busing to achieve a racial balance in schools.
     v. The police should be given more authority.
     w. President Nixon favors giving the police more authority.

x. American voters favor giving the police more authority.

y. Farmers should be guaranteed a good income.

z. President Nixon believes farmers should be guaranteed a good income.

aa. American voters favor guaranteeing farmers a good income.

bb. The government should act to stop pollution.

cc. President Nixon believes the government should act to stop pollution.

dd. American voters want the government to act to stop pollution.

ee. The federal government is getting too powerful.

ff. President Nixon believes the federal government is getting too powerful.

gg. American voters think the federal government is getting too powerful.

hh. A person who is fascinated by ideas is an effective politician.

ii. New ways of doing things usually aren't worth the effort to get them accepted.

jj. Civil servants have the narrow preoccupations of their own agencies.

kk. The federal government is too large and complex for effective coordination.

ll. Too many questions are brought to the White House for decision.

mm. The White House has adequate resources to impose presidential priorities on the government.

nn. The best way to deal with an emerging problem is to create a new federal program.

oo. Members of the White House staff have broader perspectives than those working in other agencies. [End of card sort]

Now, about your work within the Domestic Council. . .

10. Which persons do you spend the most time with in getting your own work done?

*11. Among members of the Council staff, who would you say is the *most respected?* I mean the kind of man a new member would look up to when he's just learning about the Council and how it works.

*12. Are there any staff members who are especially *expert* in their areas of Council work? Individuals who are always fully informed and particularly influential for that reason?

*13. If there is disagreement among staff members in regard to some key problem, which member's opposition would you be most concerned about?

*14. From your experience, would you say that personal friendships play an important part in the way things work? [If yes.] Whom among all the staff members do you personally like the best?

Now let's talk a bit about your relationships with the agencies.

*15. Many discussions of government say decisions are made through bargaining. Does this go on within or between the agencies you've dealt with? [If yes.] Could you explain a bit just what this bargaining implies? [If no.] If there is no bargaining, what other ways are there to make decisions?

†16. Once an agency has made a decision about its policy preferences, how does it go about seeking White House endorsement? What strategies are available to it?

†17. Once a presidential decision has been made about a given policy, how do you go about obtaining agency support for it? What strategies are available to you?

And a couple of points on your own background. . .

18. How were you recruited for this position?

19. Were you at all involved in politics prior to this appointment? [If yes.] When did you first become active? Were you involved in the 1960 Nixon campaign in any way? Were you involved in the 1968 Nixon campaign in any way?

We're just about done now. Do you have time for two more general questions?

20. Of all the things a president does, what do you think are the most crucial to the success or failure of an administration?

21. And what would you like to do after you leave the Domestic Council staff?

Index

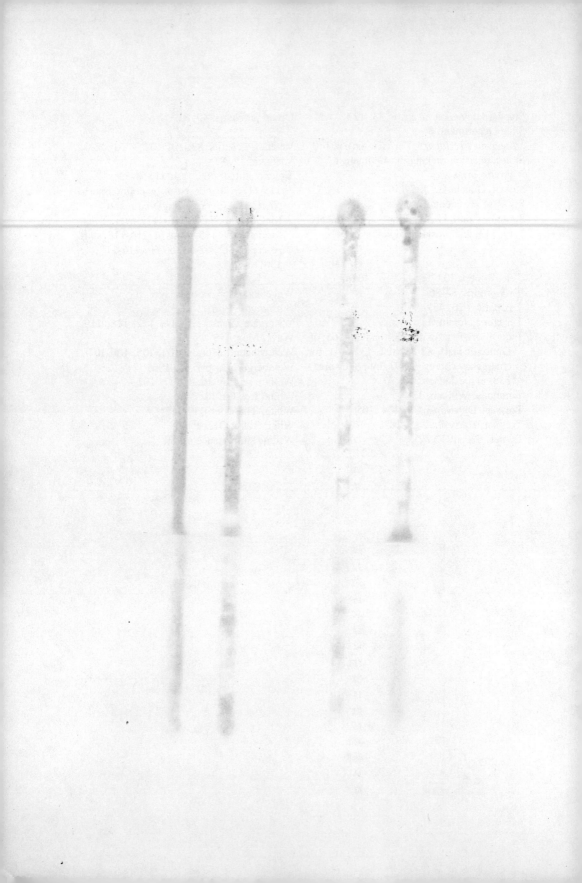